COMPETITIVE BEHAVIORS
OF
OLYMPIC GYMNASTS

CHARLES C THOMAS · PUBLISHER
Springfield · Illinois · U.S.A.

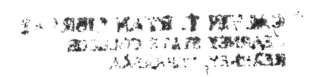

COMPETITIVE
BEHAVIORS OF
OLYMPIC GYMNASTS

By

JOHN H. SALMELA, Ph.D.

Research Chairman
Canadian Gymnastics Federation
Département d'Education Physique
Université de Montréal
Montréal, P.Q., Canada

with

Bernard Petiot, M.Sc.
Université Laval
Québec P.Q., Canada

Madeleine Hallé, M.Sc.
Université Laval
Québec, P.Q., Canada

Guy Régnier, M.Sc.
Université de Montréal
Montréal, P.Q., Canada

Published and Distributed Throughout the World by

CHARLES C THOMAS • PUBLISHER

BANNERSTONE HOUSE

301-327 East Lawrence Avenue, Springfield, Illinois, U.S.A.

© *1980 by* CHARLES C THOMAS • PUBLISHER

ISBN 0-398-04019-2 Cloth

ISBN 0-398-04021-4 Paper

Library of Congress Catalog Card Number: 79-26433

With THOMAS BOOKS *careful attention is given to all details of
manufacturing and design. It is the Publisher's desire to present
books that are satisfactory as to their physical qualities and artistic
possibilities and appropriate for their particular u*se. THOMAS
BOOKS *will be true to those laws of quality that assure a good
name and good will.*

Printed in the United States of America

N-11

Library of Congress Cataloging in Publication Data

Salmela, John H.
    Competitive Behaviors of Olympic Gymnasts.

    Bibliography: p.
    Includes indexes.
    1. Gymnastics—Psychological aspects.   2. Olympic Games,
Montréal, Québec, 1976. I. Title.
GV461.5.S24   796.4'1   79-26433
ISBN 0-398-04019-2 Cloth
ISBN 0-398-04021-4 Paper

To other people watchers in sport

PREFACE

THE STAGING of the Olympic Games every four years is a universal stimulus for all of the countries of the world to present upon a common platform their athletic elite, in order to push back the restraining margins limiting the attainment of human perfection in sport. The host country of each Olympiad, even when heavily burdened with political, administrative, and financial problems, often inherits, as a result of collective toil, new sport facilities, mass transit systems, and urban renewal projects. In addition to the tangible Olympic by-products, there often occurs a collective reflection on the people of the host country. These brief moments in the international spotlight often result in greater national unity for the country in question. While this legacy may be less spectacular than the winning of gold medals, it is none the less real. Invariably, these moments of reflection on sport excellence have their most positive and dramatic effects on the domestic policies towards mass participation in physical education and elite development in sport, as well as the advances in the physical activity sciences.

The stimulus for these educational, cultural, and scientific activities was given to Canada when the city of Montreal was awarded the twenty-first Olympiad in the year 1976. Even two years prior to the actual Olympic Games, academic initiatives were carried out as a means of gathering sport-specific information of a scientific and academic nature (Salmela, 1976b). At about the same time in this pre-Olympic period, a Frenchman, Robert Mérand proposed to a group of Québec physical education specialists that this unique sporting occasion would provide a potential source of information that could lead to innovation in the teaching of physical activity. From this initial contact, a fact-finding delegation was sent to Paris in November 1974 in order to in-

vestigate the possibilities of a collaboration in such a project between France and Québec. A Franco-Québécois Collective for the
observation of the Olympic Games was formed at that time in a
variety of sport disciplines. The Government of Québec,
Haut Commissariat à la Jeunesse, aux Loisias et aux Sports,
(H.C.J.L.S.), the Office Franco-Québécois pour la Jeunesse, the
Association des Professionnels de l'Activité Physique du Québec,
and the Fédération Sportive et Gymnique du Travail (F.S.G.T.)
of France collaborated financially and materially in the project,
which was carried out over a three year period from 1975 to 1977.

During the pre-Olympic period a delegation of Québec teachers, coaches, and researchers visited the members of the F.S.G.T.
in Sète, France, in order to establish ground rules for the collaboration. Finding a common philosophical and scientific base was
difficult for systematic observation between these two Francophone
cultures that have been separated geographically for over 300
years. This problem was magnified by the great diversity of
Olympic sport activities studied, which resulted in only indirect
collaboration between the two cultures. That is, the Québec
specialists, for the most part, set out observation strategies that
differed from their French colleagues. Also, different approaches
within both the French and Québec delegations were adopted in
relation to each of the selected sports. During the Olympic
Games the French delegation came to Montreal for the observations, and one year later, both groups reassembled again in Sète to
share their findings.

The specific nature of the sport of artistic gymnastics lent itself
to the integral recording of the athletic performances by means of
film. It was then decided that, since a large number of cameras
would already be focused upon the same gymnasts, doing the same
would result only in more redundancy. Thus, a more ambitious
project was attempted by which the preparatory behaviors of the
gymnasts, as well as those that followed each performance, would
be integrally recorded. Such procedures had been already studied
to a lesser degree in teaching situations both in the classroom and
in the gymnasium.

It was believed that the accurate recording of how a gymnast
prepared for competion, the type of reaction resulting from the

performance, and the nature of the association with teammates during both the pre– and postcompetitive phases would be instructive for sport psychologists, teachers, coaches, and gymnasts attempting to understand this level of excellence. Further, it was the opinion of the authors that these competitive behavior patterns of a nontechnical nature could be different, depending upon the sex, the level of performance, and the society of origin of the gymnast.

The results of these observations of the competitive process in elite gymnastics form the contents of this book, an area that is unique in sport psychology. It is hoped that this small legacy from over 700 individual periods of observation of the competitive process, when appropriately regrouped and analyzed, will allow greater insights to be made on the nature of the human striving for excellence in this Olympic setting.

J.H.S.
B.P.
M.H.
G.R.

ACKNOWLEDGMENTS

THE PRESENT VOLUME is the result of an international project of cooperation between the Province of Québec of Canada and the Republic of France, that took place in conjunction with the twenty-first Olympiad in the city of Montreal in the year 1976. The collaboration of the Association des Professionnels de l'Activité Physique du Québec, the Office Franco-Québécois pour la Jeunesse, the Haut-Commissariat à la Jeunesse, aux Loisirs et aux Sports of the Government of Québec and the Fédération Sportive et Gymnique du Travail in France was essential for this attempt at going beyond mere spectator observation of the disciplines in the Olympic Games. The financial, material, travel and spiritual support of the above organizations personified the Olympic ideal of participating for the common good of sport and mankind. The Université de Montréal research fund (CAFIR) also facilitated the documentation for this final report.

While the work within each selected sport discipline was carried out independently, in the true Gallic fashion, the guidance of the overall project by Robert Mérand of the F.S.G.T. and Jacques Samson of Université Laval was appreciated. Our gymnastic colleagues and friends from France, Messieurs Jacques Journet and Yves Saovi, are also thanked for their frank discussion of ideas on gymnastics in a manner that exemplified international sharing and caring. The close collaboration of our associates Gaétan Laroche and Nicole Rousseau during the formative and data collection phases was essential to the completion of this project. Finally, the efforts of all of the members of the Collectif Franco-Québécois are warmly remembered in this initial attempt at pedagogical innovation that took place both in Sète, France and in Montreal, Canada.

Scientific, academic, technical and moral support from Dr.

Jean Brunelle of Université Laval, Dr. Wayne Halliwell and Dr. Georges Larivière of the Université de Montréal, Dr. Terry Orlick of Université d'Ottawa and Dr. Ted Wall of the University of Alberta were essential for this venture into the unknown in the study of elite sport behavior.

The loving care of behavior specialist Sheila Salmela during both the nurturing and preparation phases of this document provided the emotional glue for keeping the project in a cohesive state.

Finally, the meticulous and specialized technical work of Madame Françoise Brassard and Monsieur Normand Montagne of the Laboratoire de l'Homme en Mouvement du Département d'Education Physique de l'Université de Montréal facilitated the production of the final manuscript.

J.H.S.
B.P.
M.H.
G.R.

CONTENTS

COMPETITIVE BEHAVIORS
OF
OLYMPIC GYMNASTS

PART ONE

Chapter 1

A NOVEL APPROACH TO THE OBSERVATION OF GYMNASTIC BEHAVIORS

The Montreal Olympic Games' symbol of perfection: Nadia Comaneci.

Summary

In this chapter, the importance of the accurate recording of sport behaviors of a nontechnical nature is outlined
as an essential but neglected area of sport psychology.
The conceptual model of applied behavior analysis is outlined as a complementary tool to experimental research.
Using the sport setting of gymnastics at the 1976 Montreal
Olympic Games, the various methods of subject sampling,
behavior coding and decoding, and data analysis used in this
study are presented. The behavioral patterns of the competing gymnasts and the comparisons across the sex, the
performance level, and the society of origin of the performers are outlined.

INTRODUCTION

THE SCENARIO UNFOLDS during an Olympic gymnastics competition in the Montreal Forum, the hockey shrine of professional
sports' most successful team, the Montreal Canadiens. Ludmilla
Tourischeva of the Soviet Union, defending world and Olympic
champion, paces back and forth for seven and a half minutes in
front of her team bench, oblivious to teammates, who are warming
up for the compulsory balance beam competition. Tourischeva
does not watch her teammates who are competing; nor does she
watch Nadia Comaneci, Rumanian *wunderkind*, scoring a perfect
10 on the uneven parallel bars; nor does she congratulate Olga
Korbut, the darling of the Munich Olympics, for her 9.8 score on
the beam; nor does she talk with or even approach the Soviet
Union's floor coach; nor does she physically warm up for the
routine she has practiced for at least four years. She just paces
back and forth, thinking of the task at hand.

When her competition number is flashed on the scoreboard,
her pacing stops and she approaches the 4 inch beam and begins
the routine. But something is wrong. The Queen of Gymnastics
is wobbling uncharacteristically during her normally flawless performance. Upon dismounting, she bows formally but without
emotion to the head judge and returns to the bench. No one approaches her with a word of acknowledgment, a pat on the back,
or even a nod of the head. She drapes her C.C.C.P. jacket over
her shoulders and begins her pacing again. She does not see that

a 9.4 score has been flashed and thus does not react emotionally to the deliberations of her evaluators. Probably her body's kinesthetic system has already signaled her brain that a 9.4 score would be flashed based on countless previous evaluations. Tourischeva regroups with the other team members, and they march the 25 meters to the next team bench for the floor exercises. After her brief three-minute warm-up on the Reuther floor, she will begin again her pacing.

Five rows up in the premium red seats of the Montreal Forum, a behavior evaluator is timing and recording every action of Tourischeva's preparation ritual, her relationship with her associates before and after the performance, and her observable emotional reactions to the performance and to the score that was flashed. Four other evaluators are visually following, timing, and recording the competitive behaviors of Ludmilla's teammates Nelli Kim and Olga Korbut, Rumania's Nadia Comaneci, and East Germany's Angelika Hellmann, according to a schedule determined the night before.

While the trained gymnastic judges record the movement behaviors of the gymnasts on the four women's events and then generate a mark that demonstrates how closely the performances approximate the exacting gymnastic criteria set down in the *Code of Points,* the behavior evaluators are limited, for the moment, to the accurate recording of all pre– and postcompetitive behaviors of these same gymnasts. One month later the recording sheets will be coded into numbers and words that a *Control Data®* computer can understand. One year later all statistical analysis will have been completed. However, a final evaluation comparable to Tourischeva's 9.4 cannot be flashed, since no *Code of Points* exists that tells the evaluators how close to perfection were the competitive behaviors of Ludmilla Tourischeva when she was not wobbling on the balance beam.

The evaluators do believe, however, when all analyses are terminated on the over 700 performances that were observed, that reference points for behavioral standards in Olympic gymnastics competition will help gymnasts, coaches, and other behavioral evaluators to better understand the competitive process in sport. Will certain tendencies emerge when these observations are regrouped for comparisons from one ability level to another, from one society to another, or from one sex to the other? At this time, only hunches exist, since little behavioral data on sport can be found.

This is an untraditional form of research in the young area of sport psychology. It is also one that Wolcott (1975) terms ethnographic, a field of study that is high in its risk, and potentially low in its yield, since one is never sure what will come out of the computer one year after the event. Greater difficulty will occur in the attempt to attach meaning to these behaviors. Still, explanation and prediction in science must wait the initial step of accurate description. It is the description of the competitive behaviors of Olympic gymnasts that is the purpose of this book.

CONCEPTUAL ORIENTATION

While experimental research directed to theoretical model testing has held a privileged position in sport psychology, this orientation is not the sole means of study open to investigators. The relatively new area in psychology of applied behavior analysis, as outlined by Baer, Wolf, and Risley (1968), is differentiated from basic reductionist research in terms of the emphasis on and the selection of the problem to be studied. The desire to generate behavioral changes in real-world situations constrains applied behavioral analysis to ". . . behaviors which are socially important, rather than convenient for study" (Baer, Wolf, & Risley, 1968). This paradigmatic shift to analysis of behaviors within a more natural setting is justified by the fact that the laboratory environment is rarely one in which important social behaviors can take place. This increased correspondence between the real world and the phenomenon under investigation, however, is offset by a decrease in experimental control. This and other issues that relate to applied behavior analysis are presented by Rushall (1978) in an attempt to justify this method as a useful tool for the practitioner in physical activity. Even behavioral research of the Skinnerian variety is judged to be constrained when compared to the naturalistic ethological viewpoint. It is argued that controlled behavioral analysis may be at the present time premature until the range of human behaviors and their functional importance are better known.

If the current research in sport psychology is distributed along a continuum ranging from the tightly experimental variety to natural observation, the greatest bulk falls clearly at the experimental extreme, at least in North America. For example, the concepts of motivation, personality, and anxiety are often the themes of study in sport psychology research and are put to theoretical scrutiny in the laboratory using refined tools often originating from experimental psychology (Alderman, 1974). These constructs, in some isolated cases, have also been investigated behaviorally in sport situations. The communication and feedback patterns of minor league hockey (Brunelle, Talbot, Tousignant, Hubert & Ouellet, 1978) and baseball coaches (Smoll, Smith & Hunt, 1974), as well as of a top level basketball coach (Tharp & Gallimore, 1976) have recently been observed and related to current theoretical views. However, high level sport performance and its psychological prerequisites have not received the attention by sport psychology researchers across this wide spectrum of analytical viewpoints. Most research has been confined to the determination of the personality substrates found in high level competitors in different disciplines (Vanek, Hosek, & Svoboda, 1974). Situation-specific characteristics of the anxiety levels of athletes in the different phases of competition have also been considered by Martens (1977) using a brief questionnaire. Only in rare cases (Genov, 1974) have the actual behaviors during the competitive situation been integrally recorded in a manner that is comparable to the ethological techniques used in the study of animal and human behaviors in natural settings. Studies related to the assessment of human behaviors in sport and their subsequent modification have enjoyed a somewhat greater resurgence in the total sport psychology picture (Rushall, 1978), though these advances are modest in comparison with the volume of experimental analysis.

The integral recording of those behaviors that occur during the preperformance and the postperformance periods of Olympic gymnastic competitions was the goal of this observational project. Using a behavioral assessment technique that resembled interval recording (Kazdin, 1975), the dynamic patterns of preparatory psychological and physical behaviors and emotional states were recorded, along with the corresponding social states of each athlete during the four-minute period preceding the gymnastic event. The type and source of the feedback that the gymnast received upon dismounting from the apparatus were also recorded, along with the type of emotional response to the performance and to its evaluation.

A. Preparation

B. Social State

C. Performance

D. Affective Reaction   E. Feedback   F. Affective
(Performance)   Reaction
(Evaluation)

Figure 1-1. The chronological depiction of the competition behaviors of the Olympic gymnasts observed in this study.

METHODS AND PROCEDURES
Subjects

A total of 159 elite gymnasts, 73 males and 86 females, were observed during six days of competition at the 1976 Montreal Olympic Games. All competing female gymnasts and 81.1% of the participating male gymnasts were observed for at least one performance, and in some cases for every performance, so that observations were made on 90.3% of the total gymnastic population competing at this event. Of the 2153 gymnastic routines performed, 714, or 33.2%, were included in these observations.

While all of the females from each of the 18 participating countries were observed, only male gymnasts from 18 of the 20 competing nations were studiable. Lone gymnasts from Denmark and Israel were not in the observed sample. In the preliminary compulsory and optional routines of Competition 1, in which every gymnast competes, a wide variety of gymnasts was chosen for observation to provide a broad base of ability levels and nationalities in the analysis. In the all-around finals of Competition 2, in which only the top 36 men and women compete, the gymnasts were preselected to maintain this wide base of observations, while the projected winners of the individual events were also included. In the finals for the individual events in Competition 3, where the highest scoring six gymnasts on each of the ten events compete, all performers were observed.

Recording Procedures

Five experienced gymnastic specialists, three males and two females, elaborated the observation strategy for the analysis based upon a pilot study using American male gymnasts. The actual instrument used for observation was tested during the pre-Olympic dress rehearsal one week prior to the competition in order to establish consensus reliability between the observers by simultaneously evaluating the same gymnast. Consensus on the perception of the defined behaviors between observers was established by means of comparing independent evaluations on the same gymnast and by the subsequent honing of the operational definitions for greater precision (Baer, Wolf, & Risley, 1968).

During Competitions 1 and 2 a single observer was assigned to each predetermined gymnast to ensure the largest possible number of observations on different gymnasts. During Competition 3 each gymnast was observed by two experimenters, so that the criterion of agreement of 80% between the two observations could be calculated (Hall, 1974) based upon 84 parallel observations. Prior to the competition, each observer was assigned six of the 12 gymnasts from the official event rotation sheets. This allowed every second gymnast on the order sheet to be observed by one person continuously during the whole pre– and postcompetitive period. Thus, two observers could trace the behaviors of every gymnast at one particular station. All observers had an excellent vantage point within close proximity to each other throughout the six days of competition.

The observations were pooled over the six days of competition and were regrouped and analyzed across the independent variables of sex, performance level, and society of origin of the gymnast. Five levels of performance were maintained based upon approximately equal numbered groups of scores within the brackets of 9.0, 9.0–9.3, 9.35–9.5, 9.55–9.75, and 9.8–10. The gymnasts from the 18 participating countries were regrouped again into approximately equal numbers within broad societal classifications having cultural affinities in the following manner: Anglophones (Australia, Canada, England, United States) ; Germans (German Democratic Republic, German Federal Republic) ; eastern Europeans (Bulgaria, Czechoslovakia, Hungary, Poland, Rumania) ; western Europeans (Belgium, France, Holland, Italy, Spain, Switzerland). Mexico was included with the western Europeans because of its Latin nature, while Japan and the Soviet Union had sufficient numbers of observations to remain by themselves.

Coding of Behaviors

An observation recording sheet was specifically designed in order to gather a set of behavioral data on each selected gymnast. The recording sheet, once completed, enabled each observation to be specifically identified in terms of the type of competition, the event, the order of competition on the team, the score, the placing, the name of the gymnast, and the country of origin. Any of these variables could have been used as variables for later comparisons, but only the sex of the gymnast, the score level, and the society of the gymnast were retained.

The diverse forms of behavior over a time period were recorded using the behavioral analysis techniques of event recording and time sampling described by Sidman (1960). An example of an actual observation sheet is shown in figure 1-2. Here is recorded the preparatory and social behavioral profile, the post-competitive emotional reactions to the performance and to the score, and the type and source of performance feedback for Nadia Comaneci's competitive behavior portrait surrounding her gold medal winning performance on the balance beam.

The type of competition, the event, and the other relevant identification indices of this observation are shown along the upper border. In this case, it can be seen that gymnast number 73, Nadia Comaneci, from Rumania, competed fourth during the finals, finished first on this event and first all-around. Most of this information was filled in for all of each observer's sheets prior to the competition. The perfect score of 10.00 and her placings were added after the competition, based upon the results of the official score sheets.

In the main area of the recording sheet, in Section I, entitled "Preparation," is a list of the behaviors that were anticipated, based upon a pretest at the NCAA gymnastics competition in 1975 in Philadelphia. The duration of each behavior was recorded in the space next to the appropriate behavior. The observer initiated an *Omega*® digital stopwatch at the beginning of the observation of the selected gymnast. If and when the behavior changed, the stopwatch was put on "lap time," and the frozen displayed time was recorded in the appropriate space. The watch was then pressed again and continued to record the duration of the next behavior. The actual duration of each behavior was calculated by subtracting the length of time for that behavior from the one immediately to its left. This was done after the competition was over.

Using the symbols under Section II, "Social," the type and duration of the social state of the gymnast during the preparation

PROJECT GYM 76 (MONTREAL OLYMPICS)

COMPETITION: 1ₐ 1_b 2 ③ EVENT ♂ ♀   F.X. P.H. V R P.B.   COMP. ORDER: 1 2 3 ④ 5 6   NUMBER: # 43

OBSERVER: SAL   V. U.P.B. Ⓑ F.X.   POSITION: EVENT _1_ TOTAL _1_   GYMNAST: COMANECI   COUNTRY: RUMANIA

TIME

II. SOCIAL STATES	I. PREPARATION BEHAVIORS	74	12	16	11	16	20	14	7
	PASSIVE	***							
	responsive		102						170
	concentration								
	ACTIVE	***							
	physical warm-up					129			
ALONE:	ideomotor (part)								
TEAM: T	ideomotor (whole)								
COACH: C	manipulation	86							
ADVERSARY: A	locomotion			113		149	163		
COPRESENCE: —	activation								
INTERACTION: O	relaxation								
	other (specify)	74 (PACING)							

III. FEEDBACK

	IV. AFFECTIVE REACTION	PERF.	SCORE
☐ information	nothing		
☑ positive	positive	✓	✓
☐ negative	negative		
☐ nothing			

Ⓒ = Coach
T = Teammate
Ⓐ = Adversary

REMARKS

10.00 Perfect Score!
Gold Medal!!

Figure 1-2. The observation sheet on which were recorded Nadia Comaneci's competitive behaviors prior to and following her gold medal performance on the balance beam.

phase could also be recorded.   The type and source of feedback and the affective or emotional state of the gymnast were recorded in Sections III and IV of the observation sheet, respectively.

In this case, Nadia's first behavior observed was that of pacing to and fro for 74 seconds, recorded in the "other" section.   Since no other symbols from the "social" section accompanied this number, this meant that she was alone for this duration, as she was during the whole observation period.   Her competitive behavior profile was as follows: 74 seconds of pacing to and fro, 12 seconds of equipment manipulation, 16 seconds of passive observation of the competition, 11 seconds of walking towards the apparatus, 16 seconds of nonspecific warm-up, 20 seconds of equipment manipulation, 14 seconds of walking towards the apparatus, and finally, 7 seconds of concentration before mounting upon the balance beam.   Full definitions of the preparatory behaviors and of the social states appear, respectively, in chapters 3 and 4.

Nadia's smile after having dismounted was recorded as a positive affective reaction to the performance.   On returning to the bench, she received positive feedback from her coach as well as from her adversaries.   Finally, once the score was flashed, it was noted that she responded positively to the perfect mark of 10.00. The chronological unfolding of the phases of the observation is shown in figure 1-1.   Full definitions of the feedback and emotional behaviors appear, respectively, in chapters 5 and 6.

Analysis of Data

All observation sheets were completed with information on scores and placings after the competition, and this information was then coded and transferred to data sheets for keypunching and data analysis.

The preparatory and social states were initially compared in order to determine the distribution of total observation times for all of the 714 performances.   It was decided that the observation durations would be truncated at four minutes prior to the competition, since 85% of all of the observations were at least four minutes in length.   The relative contributions of each of the retained behavior classifications for the preparatory and social states were evaluated by sampling the total behavior pattern every two seconds by computer.

The distributions of the feedback patterns and the affective re-actions were also calculated using descriptive statistics. All dependent variables were compared between sexes, performance levels, and societies using available computer statistical packages.

In contrast to the applied behavior analysis procedures by which the patterns of behaviors demonstrate their own significance without the aid of statistical analysis (Baer, Wolf, & Risley, 1968), the present data were analyzed with nonparametric statistics as a means of highlighting these tendencies and satisfying inquisitive sport psychologists.

STRUCTURE OF THE BOOK

The book is organized in three parts. Part One includes this initial chapter, along with chapter 2 on the Fundamental Demands of Gymnastic Performance. Part Two includes four chapters that describe, in a nearly chronological order, the four major behavior classifications retained in this study, that is, precompetitive preparatory (chapter 3) and social behaviors (chapter 4), feedback patterns (chapter 5) , and emotional reactions (chapter 6) .

Part Three is made up of global comparisons of all retained behaviors between men and women (chapter 7) and between the societies from which the gymnasts originated (chapter 8) . In chapter 9, a brief retrospective look is taken at the overall project and its implications and applications in the worlds of sport and sport psychology. Each chapter is followed by several Points of Interest, which can be used to stimulate thought or to highlight new directions that could be taken.

Chapter 2

FUNDAMENTAL DEMANDS OF GYMNASTIC PERFORMANCE

Similar movements on different gymnastic events.

Summary

In this chapter, a justification for the analysis of gymnastic task demands and a gymnast's prerequisite abilities is given. The direct and indirect constraints of the sport are examined as a function of the rule structure and the physical design of the equipment. A model of gymnastic performance is presented, outlining the relative contributions of morphological, organic, perceptual, or psychosocial determinants. Selected variables on the gymnasts competing at the Montreal Olympics are compared to those from the Munich Games, and their repercussions on the other gymnastics behaviors are discussed.

O NE UNIQUE FEATURE of this book on the sport of gymnastics is that it does not analyze the primary subject that is considered in most gymnastics books, that is, the gymnastic movements themselves. This task of movement analysis is accomplished with the most eloquence in the recent milestone book on the mechanics of gymnastics by George (1980). What, then, is the point of talking about gymnastics without referring to gymnastics technique? Further, why does an analysis of all of the competitive behaviors surrounding gymnastic performance have to make more than a passing reference to the demands of the sport? Perhaps a mundane example at this point might justify this procedure.

Imagine that you are applying for the unlikely job on the bomb squad for deactivating terrorist explosives. In the first place, you would probably begin to study just what are the task demands of this very highly paid job. You would inform yourself of the various dimensions of the job at hand, such as the consequences of error based possibly upon the percentage of total fatalities, or the percentage of fatalities through human error. Further, you would try to find out just what has to be done in order to succeed, since the payoffs for failure are not attractive. Perhaps you would find out what manual skills are necessary to deactivate the explosives, what perceptual skills are necessary in order to read the key wiring patterns, and what intellectual skills or particular disposition is necessary in order to know how to act appropriately in any potential situation.

Once the task of bomb deactivation has been analyzed along

its most appropriate dimensions, you would probably compare your own capabilities with the demands of the task. If you have poor eyes, slow reactions, clumsy fingers, a nervous disposition, and a large protruding abdomen, you may be the wrong person for this job. But if you do possess the appropriate characteristics, you will probably take the job, and later on you may wish to work into further means of aiding your performance capabilities.

It is at this moment that you may begin to watch the other associated behaviors of some of your associates in the bomb deactivation business. How do they relax themselves to work at their greatest efficiency? Do they confer with colleagues before deactivating, do they stay isolated, do they read manuals, or do they just pray? Do they have special powder on their fingers or lead shields on their bodies? After deactivation, do they seem satisfied, indifferent, or do they continually rethink better ways of doing the job? Do they seem to receive appropriate rewards at the end of their performance to warrant the energy expended? All of these questions can be partially answered through the systematic observation of expert bomb deactivators.

And it is for these analogous reasons that the gymnastics task demands and performance capabilities are being considered prior to embarking upon a more detailed analysis of the nontechnical competitive behaviors of Olympic gymnasts.

It is essential, however, to point out that most potential gymnasts do not go through the sequence of events just described, as did the aspiring bomb deactivator. Rather, it is usually the purely fun aspects, arising from putting one's body in improbable and inhabitual positions, that initially motivate youngsters to get involved in this sport. Therefore, the following discussion is directed to the gymnast or sport scientist who is trying to explain or understand behaviors after the fact.

TASK DEMANDS OF GYMNASTICS

Gymnastics shares many performance qualities with other Olympic disciplines when observation is only limited to the overt movement patterns that are performed. For example, explosive acceleration on the vault can be compared to the effort required in the sprint events in track, while the strength requirements for the rings may match those found in wrestling or weight lifting (deGaray, Leving, & Carter, 1974). However, there appear to be more dissimilarities than similarities between gymnastics and the other classifications of activities found at the summer Olympics (Salmela, 1976a). For one thing, the variety of purely physical manipulations that the body must go through in gymnastics is much greater than those of any other discipline, the decathlon included.

However, these movement patterns in gymnastics also require enormous contributions of courage that go beyond that of propelling oneself over the 18 foot bar in pole vault. Besides attaining these same physical heights, along with the anticipation of much more rigid landing surfaces, in gymnastics this performance differs in other ways from most other sports. These predetermined complex movement patterns must also be executed with elegance and apparent ease, so that the final performance can be judged by a panel of experts. The following is a brief look at how this distinct nature of gymnastics uniquely taxes the performance capacities of the gymnast.

The rules and regulations that guide gymnastic performance, i.e. *Code of Points* of the Fédération Internationale de Gymnastique can be considered to be *indirect constraints* of gymnastics (Arend & Higgins, 1976), since they arbitrarily spell out what can and cannot be included in a routine. For example, a handstand is possible on the pommel horse, but the rule requiring continuous movement precludes its appearance in a routine. Generally, the rules require that artistry, as exemplified by effortless performance, be the predominant performance quality. However, the men's rules also state that each gymnast must demonstrate virtuosity by showing exceptional *execution,* originality through the use of unique movement *combinations,* as well as risk by including extreme *difficulty.* Therefore, by pushing performance requirements to their utmost while at the same time requiring elegant execution, the constraints put the gymnast in the paradoxical situation of making the difficult appear easy. As Lascari (1976) points out, these *indirect constraints* are opposite to those present in the circus, where an attempt is made to have the easy appear difficult.

Aside from the *indirect constraints* of the rules, the *direct environmental constraints* of each event result in more dramatic consequences on the part of the gymnast. The physical construction of the different events in terms of their spatial configurations, the apparatus flexibility, and their relative stability are limiting factors in determining behavior. These constraints literally prevent certain movement patterns from happening, even if the *indirect constraints* of the rules permitted these behaviors. One only has to think of the feasibility of the one-handed handstand on the parallel bars as compared to the impossibility of doing the same movement on the rings. The very nature of these *direct constraints* determine movement patterns of an incredibly varied nature both in time as well as in space. In previous research (Salmela, 1976a), the effects of both the indirect and direct constraints on the type of decision making, perceptual processes, and movement requirements have been studied. It has also been shown that these various demands have increased since 1968 so that the gymnast is required to perceive things more quickly, to move faster, and to place his or her body in more and more precarious positions. Given these task demands, just what kind of human being is best fit to perform these increasingly difficult sport performances?

DETERMINANTS OF GYMNASTIC PERFORMANCE

In a similar manner to the potential bomb deactivator's decision processes in deciding on whether or not to choose this particular profession, this inquiry has progressed, as did he, through the analysis of the task demands. What now would be the most efficient way of matching these demands to the particular makeup of a potential gymnast?

Bouchard (1975) has evolved a performance model that exhaustively outlines the environmental, or variable, determinants and the hereditary, or invariable, determinants that contribute to the total variance of a given sports performance. This conceptual model attempts to delineate a means of categorizing the performance variance due either to environmental or to hereditary sources as well as to their interactions. The primary determinants are considered to be either morphological, organic, perceptual, or psychosocial in nature. With such a broad model, we can now attempt to look at the particular contributions of each class of determinant as they relate to gymnastics. It is obvious that these same relative contributions would not be the same for sport activities having other task demands (Salmela, 1979).

Figure 2-1. Dan Grecu, Rumania's world champion on the still rings, demonstrates the perceptual task of "spotting" the landing surface.

One of the most evident dimensions of gymnastic performance is the spectacular twisting, somersaulting, and maintenance of the body in controlled positions that are not encountered in everyday life activities. While this performance dimension does receive extensive consideration of a descriptive nature, little systematic research has been reported on the underlying performance mechanisms, nor of the means by which this complex skill learning takes place. These perceptual mechanisms in Bouchard's model are not very well understood, although in gymnastics they may account for the greatest performance variance. Frederick and Wilson (1973) have made to date the most elegant attempt to integrate the skill components of swinging, twisting, and somersaulting with force, balance, and flexibility elements into a model for the organization and classification of gymnastic movements.

The nature of the physiological and organic determinants that contribute most to gymnastic performance has been well delineated by Montpetit (1976). In four of the six events, explosive

Figure 2-2. The organic components of strength (left) and flexibility (right) are demonstrated by Japan's Mitsuo Tzukahara in the iron cross and split positions.

power and muscular strength are required for approximately 30 seconds, as the gymnast controls his total body weight with his hands in either support or hanging positions. These demands are such that gymnasts at a high level are among the leanest, strongest, and most flexible of all athletes (Cumming, 1967). Their vital capacity and MVO₂ levels are predictably at the lower end of the scale, and the energy costs between events are comparable (Montpetit, 1976). The high level of physiological trainability of the necessary qualities for advanced performance in gymnastics presents the most researched factor that is potentially exposed to environmental manipulation.

Advantageous morphological characteristics of gymnasts facilitate the efficient functioning of the muscular and organic qualities required for the necessary dynamic and powerful movements of short duration. Gymnasts thus tend to be smaller and lighter than most other Olympic athletes (Medved, 1966; Montpetit, 1976; Parizkova, 1972). The best teams seem to have mechanical advantages, with body dimensions that are to a great degree inherited (Bouchard, Brunelle & Godbout, 1973), such as decreased height and shorter extremities (Nelson, 1974). However, certain body types may be advantageous on certain events while a disadvantage on others.

Figure 2-3. Particular morphological demands of gymnastics are evidenced by the lean, muscled body of Hungary's Feranc Donath.

The sociopsychological determinants of gymnastic performance are less well documented than are the others. However, mastering of the complex compulsory and optional routines on the six events in order to meet the exacting requirements of the international regulations assumes a social milieu that is compatible with four to six hours of training per day. Roethlisberger (1970) has reported that elite American male gymnasts were for the most part unmarried university students or instructors willing to sacrifice social position and academic standards for excellence. The decreasing age of present-day gymnasts puts increased demands upon their educational or political systems in order to support this life-style.

The psychological qualities that are prerequisite to gymnastic performance would seem to be varied in nature, given the complex nature of the different events (Orlick, 1976). Pommel horse requires calm control and high concentration for over 30 seconds, due to the fact that the upper information processing limits seem to be reached (Salmela, 1979b), while the long horse vault re-

Figure 2-4. The individual interacts in many ways within the social milieu that is particular to gymnastics.

Figure 2-5. The psychological preparation for competition is shown by Japan's Kyoko Mano during these final moments.

quires brief but explosive performance. Other measured, but theoretically stable and independent, personality traits have been tested for in gymnasts in order to determine specific profiles for the sport (Kroll & Crenshaw, 1968; Cooper, 1969). While certain characteristics have been reported to be common to elite gymnasts, such as high intelligence, practicality, apprehension, and independence (Kroll & Crenshaw, 1968), little has been done concerning these psychological traits in regards to the actual task demands of gymnastics. Desharnais (1976) provides some evidence that Cattell's secondary personality factors may be directly related to the varied psychomotor task demands of archery, weight lifting, high jumping, and curling. Selective factors of a psychological nature may be as important as those of the structure determinants for performance at a high level.

In fact, two recent studies show that specific morphological and psychological qualities of elite gymnasts are very compatible with and possibly are determinants of successful gymnastic performance. In a study on the male Canadian Olympic aspirants, it was found that anxiety levels and certain morphological qualities were good predictors of success in gymnastics (Salmela, Hallé, Petiot, & Samson, 1978). These results of task-gymnast compatibility were supported, in part, by another study on American male gymnastic specialists who had body types and psychological predispositions that were judged to be appropriate for successful performance in their chosen gymnastic event (Salmela, Hallé, Petiot, Samson, & Biesterfeldt, 1980).

In a further attempt to predict which variables contributed most to gymnastic success at different age levels for Canadian male gymnasts (Salmela, Régnier, & Proteau, 1979), it was found that very general basic processes of athletic skill were essential at the lower age levels. These measures could be taken by simple tests of balance, speed, strength, power, and flexibility that were derived from a gymnastic application of Bouchard's model shown in figure 2-6. However, at the more elite levels, very specific qualities that required specialized equipment had to be used in order to find variables that could successfully predict performance excellence.

The general morphological characteristics of this particular

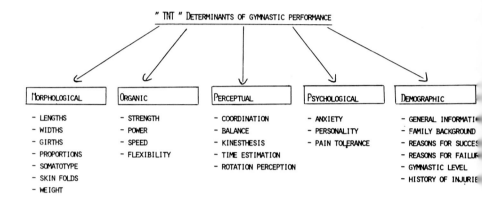

Figure 2-6. Determinants of gymnastic performance that were evaluated in a Test for National Talent (TNT) in Canada. Adapted from Bouchard, Brunelle, and Godbout (1975).

population of Olympic gymnasts at Montreal were available from the literature distributed by the organizing committee. Unfortunately, it was not possible for this whole population of athletes to undergo extensive testing specific to gymnastics. Still, the available information relating to age, height, and weight can be compared to the information that Montpetit (1976) reported on the gymnasts participating in the 1972 Munich Olympics.

The top five male gymnastic teams in Montreal were identical in order to those at Munich, with the exception that Hungary replaced Poland in the fourth position (table 2-I). For the men on these top five teams, with the exception of Japan, which maintained many of the members from the previous Olympics, the average age was lower than those gymnasts at Munich by about 1 to 1.5 years. The heights and weights of the gymnasts of these five teams tended to increase slightly. Thus, it appeared that younger, taller, and possibly more powerful male gymnasts were the most successful types at these Olympic Games.

The women, however, showed radically different tendencies than did the men. The order of the team placings was quite different from that at Munich. The Soviet Union and Czecho-

TABLE 2-I

AVERAGE AGE, HEIGHT AND WEIGHT OF THE TOP FIVE
MALE TEAMS AT THE 1976 MONTREAL OLYMPIC GAMES

| Country | Rank | By Team | | |
		Age	*Height (cm)*	*Weight (kg)*
Japan	1	27.2	167.4	59.3
Soviet Union	2	21.1	169.1	61.4
East Germany	3	22.9	169.0	63.8
Hungary	4	22.7	165.2	58.0
West Germany	5	24.2	170.1	65.0
TOTALS OF MEMBERS OF THE TOP FIVE TEAMS				
Mean[a]		23.6	167.5	61.5
Maximum		21.1	164.4	58.0
Minimum		27.2	170.6	65.0

[a]$n = 35$.

slovakia still maintained their respective first and fifth places, but
East Germany was replaced by Rumania in second place, and
they, in turn, displaced Hungary from third spot (table 2-II).
Hungary also displaced the United States from the fourth position. In comparison to Munich results, only the average age of the

TABLE 2-II

AVERAGE AGE, HEIGHT AND WEIGHT OF THE TOP FIVE
FEMALE TEAMS AT THE 1976 MONTREAL OLYMPIC GAMES

| Country | Rank | By Team | | |
		Age	*Height (cm)*	*Weight (kg)*
Soviet Union	1	19.6	154.7	43.6
Rumania	2	16.2	155.2	44.2
East Germany	3	18.9	165.1	46.5
Hungary	4	18.5	160.2	44.8
Czechoslovakia	5	16.9	159.4	49.1
TOTALS OF MEMBERS OF TOP FIVE TEAMS				
Mean[a]		18.0	158.1	45.6
Minimum		16.2	154.7	43.6
Maximum		19.6	161.1	49.1

[a]$n = 35$.

Hungarian team increased at the Montreal Games. But for every team, without exception, the average height and weight of the gymnasts were lower than those of the members of the comparable teams at Munich.

In general, there was a tendency for all of the gymnasts to be younger, smaller, and lighter than those who competed four years earlier. This phenomenon was certainly more pronounced for the women than for the men. The five-year average age difference between men and the women is believed to be a significant factor in many of the behavioral differences between the sexes that are noted in the following chapters.

POINTS OF INTEREST

• The sport of gymnastics requires that the gymnast perform a wide number of very different skills in from four to six events before a panel of judges. These skills vary greatly in kind and in number, and all must be not only difficult or risky, but also performed showing creative virtuosity, lack of apparent effort, and artistic grace.

• The specific demands of many of the individual events have been shown to evolve in terms of the new stresses that are placed upon the gymnasts, both in time and in space. This means that the relative difficulty of the various gymnastic moves is ever increasing in this sport, while other sport activities remain the same from year to year.

• Previously it had been shown at other Olympics that the successful gymnasts were very light, flexible, strong, and small as compared to other athletes. However, the increasing demands placed upon gymnasts to perform even more astounding athletic feats may also have partially caused the overall lowering of the average size and age of the gymnasts, especially with the women.

• It may be that now the nervous system, rather than the muscular system, will become the limiting factor in elite sport competition in gymnastics. Increasing demands of new and daring moves will tax the perceptual and coordination systems of the gymnasts to their limits. Further, the emotional control required to perform these difficult maneuvers in high tension situations may provide

the ultimate challenge.
* At the moment, it is not known how well the younger and younger gymnasts will be able to react to the increasing levels of competitive pressure.

PART TWO

Chapter 3

PREPARING TO COMPETE

While her teammate competes, a female gymnast rehearses one last time.

Summary

In this chapter, the precompetitive behaviors of Olympic gymnasts are elaborated. The categories of instrumental, motor, ideomotor, mental, and emotional activities were applied to the observation of gymnasts four minutes prior to competition. Male and female gymnasts differed behaviorally during the preparatory period, with the former demonstrating significantly fewer ideomotor and emotional behaviors. The intensity of observed emotional behaviors again differentiated the top scoring gymnasts from all other groups. This same dimension also was shown to be highly variable, with the Soviet gymnasts demonstrating a high incidence of emotional behaviors as compared to gymnasts from any other society.

E BERHARD GIENGER, the likeable West German 1974 world champion on the horizontal bar, followed a constant ritual before he competed on each gymnastic event at the Montreal Olympics. After having completed his warm up, he sat on the bench among his teammates and watched each of them compete. Being much superior to them, he always performed last in the six-man competition order. After each of the first four performances, he rose to his feet and warmly congratulated his colleagues. As the fifth man prepared himself to compete Gienger stood up, put on his suspenders, adjusted his gymnastic pants and slippers, chalked up, put on his hand guards, placed his warm-up jacket on his shoulders, turned his back to the competition apparatus, and concentrated on the upcoming routine with his eyes closed. On hearing the fifth competitor dismount, Gienger slipped the jacket from his shoulders, passed the just-finished teammate without acknowledging him, approached the apparatus, and awaited the head judge's signal to compete.

This ritual did not vary from event to event, nor from preliminaries to finals. In all probability, the same routine had been carried out at each competition over a number of years. By maintaining this invariant series of precompetitive behaviors, Gienger was able to interact with his teammates and then could systematically get ready for the task at hand. Not all gymnasts were so meticulous in their short-term preparation as was Gienger, and it is these variations in behaviors that will be the focus of the present chapter.

Any preparation procedures for high level performance must be carried out over an extended period of time, with minute attention accorded to the smallest detail. It is convenient to divide this long range period of preparation into two phases. These can overlap in time, but the purpose of each is quite distinct. The first phase is the *acquisition* or *learning phase,* during which the greatest portion of the coach's and gymnasts' time is spent mastering new gymnastic moves and combinations. It is during this period that skills beyond the intricate gymnastic maneuvers outlined in chapter 2 are mastered. Skills of a social nature are learned at this time, such as how to best get along with fellow gymnasts by sharing time and equipment. The powerful tool of information (technical) and sanctioning (praise or scolding) feedback is felt for the first time by gymnasts, and they, in turn, are able to use these same forces when working with and helping younger gymnasts. It is at these moments of reciprocal learning and teaching that the typical club gymnast switches back and forth between the roles of the consumer and the distributor of knowledge. While the informational feedback regarding technique is so important, the young gymnasts who help in the coaching process also find out how far a kind word can take them by enticing the other gymnasts to work longer, as well as how devastating unjust criticism can be.

Most texts on the subject of the training of gymnasts deal purely with the transfer of technique (Loken, 1977) or more generally with the physiological principles of training (Taylor, 1975). While the utility of both cannot be denied, as outlined in chapter 2, the area of the psychology of learning that deals with instructional principles and institutional management has only received infrequent consideration (Salmela, 1978; 1979f).

The second aspect of preparation relates to the *performance phase,* which concerns the moment-to-moment events that must be dealt with in order to realize high level performance on a given event at a specific competition. It is these processes that will be dealt with in detail in this chapter. The distinction is made between factors that can influence learning and those that have ergogenic (Morgan, 1972) properties, that is, that can improve performance without necessarily changing the learning process. For example, a warm muscle will perform more efficiently than a cold one as a result of a warm-up, although nothing new has been learned. Morgan deals with a number of ergogenic aids that can influence learning and performance from a long to medium term period, such as hypnosis, hormone administration, nutrition, and drugs. In relation to gymnastics, these aids have effects that are beyond the temporal scope of this study, since only the four-minute period preceding the competition is presently of concern. While this period of preparation is extremely brief, there are many different classes and intensities of observable activities that have been shown to occur within this dramatic time period (Hallé, 1978).

The observable preparatory behaviors that take place immediately prior to the competition can be regrouped into five broad categories that range from purely physical to cognitive and finally to affective behaviors. The first class of behaviors is called *instrumental activities* and relates to those physical acts that allow the gymnast to materially prepare himself to compete. Usually, these are the routinized behaviors, such as putting on equipment, transporting oneself to the apparatus, and the like, that are necessarily performed in order to compete and may be carried out in a stylized or superstitious manner (Petrie & Gregory, 1973). Sandle (1972) stated that instrumental behaviors have little psychological significance as such but are merely executed in order to change a relationship between oneself and an object.

The next two classes of preparatory behaviors make up two of the three types of warm-ups outlined by Franks (1972). The first class is that of *motor activities*, or what Franks calls indirect warm-up, in which some of the same or even completely different muscle groups than those to be used in the performance are prepared for activity. These behaviors are termed motor since they involve nonspecific movement, as compared to the next class of *ideomotor activities*, which involves the functioning of motor patterns specific to the routine to be performed. Implicit within this definition is that there is a cognitive component relating to the "idea" or internalized image of the routine, rather than the

simple repetition of specific motor acts that resemble the performance. This cognitive component has been shown to be very important to performance rehearsal (Nideffer, 1976; Kane, 1978)
and differentiates this particular set of behaviors from the "identical activities" warm-up outlined by Franks (1972). Vanek and
Cratty (1970) have shown that these behaviors also provide
efficient ways of reducing precompetitive anxiety.

The next category of preparatory behaviors is that of the
mental activities that occur without body movement, usually
within the last minutes before competition. It is at these moments
that the gymnast could be concentrating mentally upon the key
elements of the gymnastic routine. Genov (1972) has described
this precompetition concentration as a means for the mobilization
of psychological and physiological energy necessary for performance. These types of mental activities can be related to the concepts of mental practice that have been shown to be valuable
techniques in learning motor tasks (Corbin, 1972). Fewer studies
have related this concentration behavior with performance, although Nideffer (1976) would suggest that this narrowing of attention for a sport activity such as gymnastics would be helpful.

Finally, one other class of behaviors, *emotional activity,* is required in order that an exhaustive description of preparatory acts
can be made. These activities can be classified preparatory in
nature even though the emotional or affective dimensions, rather
than the physical components, are being prepared. It is well
known that a specific level of precompetitive anxiety or emotion
is appropriate for certain activities and inappropriate for others.
In addition, the particular personality of the athlete may already
be predisposed to being anxious or calm, and the importance of
a competition will tend to intensify the habitual emotional levels
that could arise under normal circumstances. Thus, the level of
emotional stress or anxiety varies greatly and must be controlled,
so that the psychological components of the performance can be
managed and prepared for in the same manner as are the physical
or muscular components. The fact that the men have six and the
women have four events with extremely different task demands
(Salmela, 1976), means that each event may require specific types
of stress management. Pommel horse and beam require precise

control, and it may be that the gymnast should be calmed down emotionally by quiet pacing. The explosive vault, however, may be best prepared for by the creation of tension by contracting or through some other form of psychological "pumping up." In most cases, due to the importance of the Olympic Games, the gymnasts would not require getting emotionally high; rather, they would seek means of controlling too much competitive anxiety.

It can be now seen that there is a progression of preparatory activities that goes from instrumental acts to general motor behaviors, then to motor and ideational activities and concentration behaviors, and finally to emotional manifestations. It is now possible to see if these combinations of motor, cognitive, and affective components change between sexes, performance levels, and societies.

Male and female gymnasts would be expected to show different patterns of preparatory activity not only because of potential biological differences, but also because of the fact that the respective tasks to be performed differ in nature. Of the four women's gymnastic events, the vault, the floor exercises, and the uneven parallel bars resemble to some extent men's vault, floor exercises, and the horizontal bar, respectively, while the balance beam is very different in nature from any event on which the men perform. The men's pommel horse, rings, and parallel bars do not, in turn, have a counterpart in any women's events. It could then be expected, in certain instances, that the men and women prepare themselves in a similar manner, while on other events they do so with quite different procedures that are specific to the task demands.

There is still some discussion in regard to whether the emotional differences found between men and women in personality testing are due to different biological or socialization processes (Alderman, 1974). Few studies, however, have attempted to look at men and women using behavioral measures (Goffman, 1979).

Do top level gymnasts prepare themselves differently than those who possess a lesser degree of ability? It may be that efficiency in short-term preparation for competition is a quality shown by the more skilled gymnasts, doing only what is necessary for maximal performance. However, this efficiency might be traded off against the increased pressures and the high expectancy of success that goes along with absolute excellence at this level of competition. Since all gymnasts at each performance level perform on the same events, the physical preparation might be expected to be similar. Greatest differences would be expected for the psychological and affective components of the preparation in light of the great stresses that must be dealt with in the rarified atmosphere of the medal contenders.

Finally, there could be differences expected in preparatory behaviors between the gymnasts from different societies, since sport is a manifestation of the values and mores of each country (Dickenson, 1976; Morton, 1970). In achievement-oriented societies such as the Soviet Union or Japan (Luschen, 1970), or power-oriented societies such as the United States, the same qualities may be transformed into the preparation behaviors of their participating gymnasts. Since play, sport, and their accompanying behaviors are cultural inventions rather than biological universals (Roberts and Sutton-Smith, 1966), it would be normal to expect that the functional preparatory as well as the social behaviors (see chapter 4) during elite competition reflect the prevailing traits, values, expectations, and degree of social control of the respective societies.

Within the above framework, it is the goal of this chapter to examine the relative contributions of the different components making up the preparatory behaviors of the Olympic gymnasts in relation to their sex, performance level, and society of origin.

RECORDING PROCEDURES

The observations reported in this chapter took place during the four-minute or longer precompetitive period in which the gymnasts readied themselves for performance on the different gymnastic events. Although some observation periods exceeded 10 minutes in length, they were all truncated at four minutes, ensuring that 85% of all performances were included for at least that duration. Observation of the social states of the gymnasts (see chapter 4) were made concurrently with the preparatory behaviors, since the former changed less frequently than the latter.

The type and duration of preparatory behaviors were the variables of interest. The 13 individual behaviors were defined within the following five classes of preparatory activities and were recorded by the methods explained in chapter 1.

Instrumental Activities

Passive Responsive Waiting

This passive behavior consisted primarily of actively watching the competition from a sitting or standing position, taking on the attitude of a spectator. This was evidenced by the observed head movements following performing gymnasts and by the giving of applause. No functional movements of any importance were exhibited.

Manipulations

These instrumental activities were precise, voluntary actions used for the adjustment of the gymnastic equipment, clothing, or other gymnastic paraphernalia. Included within these activities

Figure 3-1. The passive responsive state predominates with the American women's team as they watch the competition.

were the adjustments to the bars or beatboards; adjustments to the hand guards, gymnastic pants, suspenders, leotards, or slippers; or the application of magnesium sulfate to the hands or resin to the slippers.

Locomotion

The goal of these activities was the transport of the gymnast to a precise location by walking or running. This included walking to the chalk box for magnesium sulfate or to the apparatus to compete. Locomotion was considered as the accomplishment of a precise task and thus was differentiated from pacing. Very often locomotion and manipulation occurred together.

Figure 3-2. Rumania's Theodora Ungureanu chalks up (manipulation) while approaching the apparatus (locomotion).

Waiting

This behavior occurred with the gymnast standing up in an attentive state, usually awaiting either the flashing of a score or the signal of the head judge to begin the routine.

Motor Activities

These activities were nonspecific warm-up behaviors that did not resemble the movements to be performed on the next gymnastic event. These general movements were probably used to increase the body temperature or maintain general flexibility of parts or the whole body and included jogging, hopping, skipping, rotating of limbs, twisting, stretching, or swinging of body parts. The rhythms were different than those of the routines, and they were carried out with little concern for good gymnastic form.

Figure 3-3. The United States' Jay Whelan loosens up (physical warm-up) in his own particular fashion.

Ideomotor Activities

Partial Executions

The nature of these activities was the execution of a portion of a gymnastic movement that would be performed later in the routine. These behaviors were usually executed at the same speed as those of the routine and appeared to be key elements, or kinesthetic reminders to the gymnasts of the anticipated feeling of certain key elements of the routine. Included within this category of physical and ideational preparation were placing of the arms for twisting or the setting of the arms for a cross or a handstand while not performing the rest of the movement.

Figure 3-4. The Dutch gymnasts rehearse small parts (partial execution) and the whole routine (global execution) prior to competing on the balance beam.

Global Executions

Inclusion within this category of behaviors required that the gymnast rehearse integrally whole sections of the to-be-performed routine. These rehearsals might take place on a line on the floor prior to competing on the balance beam or by turning and swivel-ling while standing up prior to pommel horse execution.

Mental Activities

Inclusion within this category required that the gymnast be immobile, either with closed eyes or with a fixed gaze that was not reactive to external stimuli. It was assumed that at these moments the gymnast was concentrating on certain key aspects of the up-coming routine.

Figure 3-5. Eberhard Gienger of West Germany readies himself mentally (concentration) for the difficult pommel horse event.

Emotional Activities

Relaxation

Activities in this category were characterized by loose shaking or swinging of the limbs, which would result in flaccidity of the limbs and other parts of the body. In certain instances this relaxa-tion of the whole body occurred by lying down on the floor in a supine position.

Activation

Behaviors in this category were brisk contracting movements, such as rapid hand clenching, arm contraction, or dynamic jumping, the purpose of which appeared to be the heightening of the general activation level of the body through increased body tension.

Nervous Tics

This class of activities was made up of small movements having no precise function but representative of a heightened state of stress. Included in these behaviors were the rapid shrugging of shoulders, twitching of the neck, biting of the lips and cheeks, turning of fingers, or rotating of the ankles.

Pacing

Activities in this category were characterized by repetitive walking to and fro across the warm-up area with no purpose of locomotion to a precise spot but rather as a means of releasing nervous tension.

The percent of agreement between the five observers for the preparatory behaviors was calculated based upon time samples every 15 seconds of the four-minute period for 88 parallel observations. The consensus between observers was 75%, the lowest percentage of agreement that was found in the project. The reason that this consensus was marginally below the 80% criteria set by Hall (1974) was partially due to the difficulty in synchronizing stopwatches in this time series observation.

SEX

The dynamic patterns for the five precompetitive behavior classifications that occurred during the four minutes that preceded the performance are given for the male and female gymnasts in figure 3-7. The greatest proportion of behaviors are the instrumental ones (67.3%), with no significant differences being found between the sexes. Similar contributions for motor behaviors (6.7%), as well as for concentration (10.5%), were observed between the male and female gymnasts. The females did demonstrate a significantly greater number of precompetitive emo-

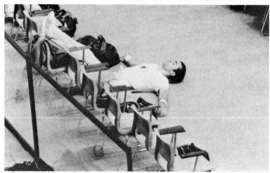

Figure 3-6. Emotional control is maintained in different manners by Ludmilla Tourischeva of the Soviet Union (pacing—upper photograph) and by
Eberhard Gienger (relaxation—lower photograph).

tional behaviors than did the male gymnasts; that is, 13.9% as
compared to 6.6% (χ^2 (9) = 39.8, $p < .01$). There was also a
greater number of ideomotor behaviors observed for the female
(6.9%) than for the male (2.1%) gymnasts (χ^2 (5) = 34.7, $p < .01$).
Temporally, it can be seen that the highest incidence of emotional
behaviors occurs two minutes prior to competing and that a high
incidence of mental behaviors of concentration occurs in the last
15 seconds.

MEN

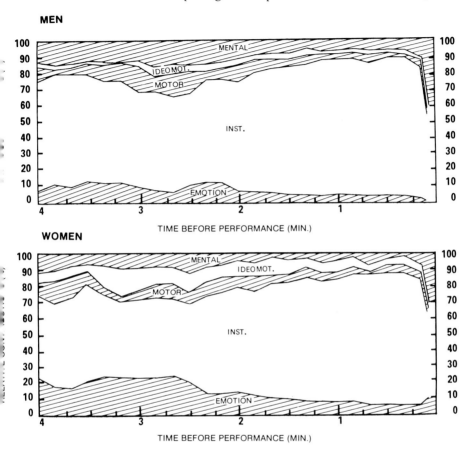

WOMEN

Figure 3-7. The relative contributions of the mental, ideomotor (ideomot.), motor, instrumental (inst.), and emotional (emotion) behavior of men and women are shown. The greater incidence of ideomotor and emotional behaviors is to be noted for the women in these profiles of precompetitive preparatory behaviors.

PERFORMANCE LEVEL

The patterns of preparatory behaviors for the five different performance levels are seen in figures 3-8 and 3-9. Comparisons between the different levels of performance and the emotional behaviors reveal that they are statistically different (χ^2 (4) = 21.24, $p < .01$). The most significant contributor to these overall differences was the extremely high incidence of emotional behaviors in the highest performance bracket of 9.8 to 10.0.   No differences were found between the performance levels for either the mental, motor, ideomotor, or instrumental behaviors.

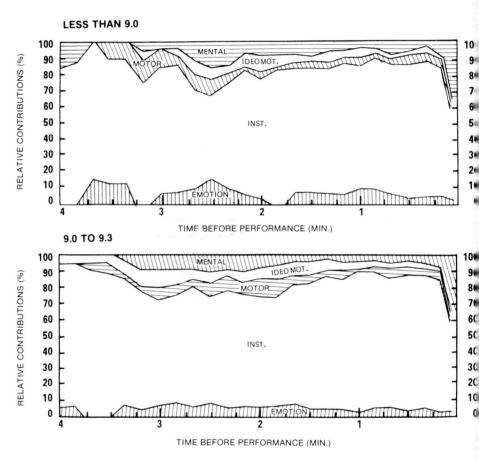

Figures 3-8 and 3-9. The greater incidence of emotional behaviors by the 9.8 to 10.0 performance group is the most striking feature of these behavior profiles of gymnasts of different performance levels.

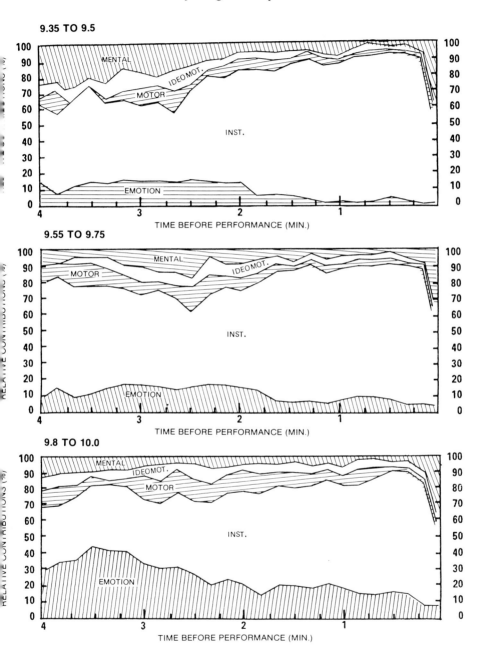

Figure 3-9.

SOCIETY

The dynamic patterns for the five precompetitive behavior classifications that occurred during the four minutes preceding the performance are shown for the Anglophone, Japanese, and western European gymnasts in figure 3-10 and for the eastern European, German, and Soviet athletes in figure 3-11. The instrumental behaviors make up the greatest portion of all gymnastic preparatory behaviors from each society, with variations between 51.9% for the Soviets up to 74.6% for the Germans. No statistically significant differences between societies were found for this variable.

Further, no differences were found between the societies for the behavior categories of mental, ideomotor, and motor activities, which respectively made up 10.5%, 4.4%, and 6.7% of the total observed behaviors. Only the category of emotional behaviors was shown to have differed significantly between societies (χ^2 (5) = 313.5, $p < .01$). The Soviet gymnasts demonstrated by far the greatest percentage of emotional behaviors (25.0%), more than twice the contribution for the closest group, the eastern Europeans (11.8%). The western European (2.6%) and German (4.9%) gymnasts demonstrated the lowest percentage of emotional behaviors.

DISCUSSION

Probably the most remarkable feature of the preparatory procedures of these Olympic gymnasts was the great similarity of most selected behaviors when compared between sexes, performance levels, and societies. The exception was the emotional behavior variable, which proved to be the most discriminating between the groups of all of the variables.

Before looking at the comparisons between the major variables, it should be noticed how the different classes of behaviors were generally distributed.

The instrumental behaviors have understandably the most frequent type of behavior during this important short-term period of preparation. Due to the highly technical nature of a sport that involves from four to six events, depending upon the sex, various

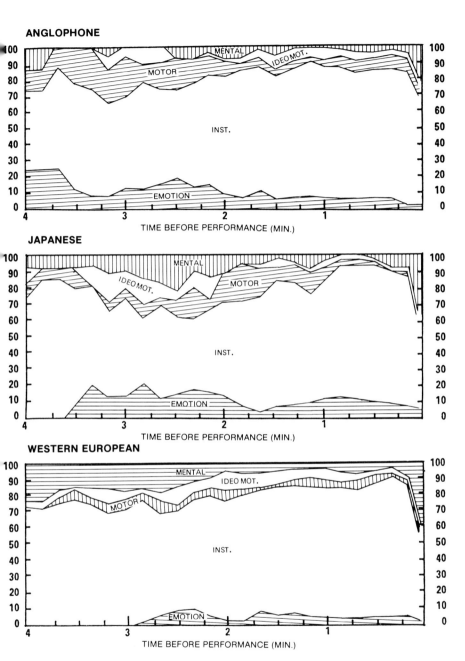

ANGLOPHONE

MENTAL
IDEO MOT.
MOTOR
INST.
EMOTION

TIME BEFORE PERFORMANCE (MIN.)

JAPANESE

MENTAL
IDEO MOT.
MOTOR
INST.
EMOTION

TIME BEFORE PERFORMANCE (MIN.)

WESTERN EUROPEAN

MENTAL
IDEO MOT.
MOTOR
INST.
EMOTION

TIME BEFORE PERFORMANCE (MIN.)

Figures 3-10 and 3-11. The preparation patterns between societies of all observed behaviors are similar except for those behaviors classified as being emotional. The high incidence of these behaviors by the Soviets should be noted in comparison to the western Europeans.

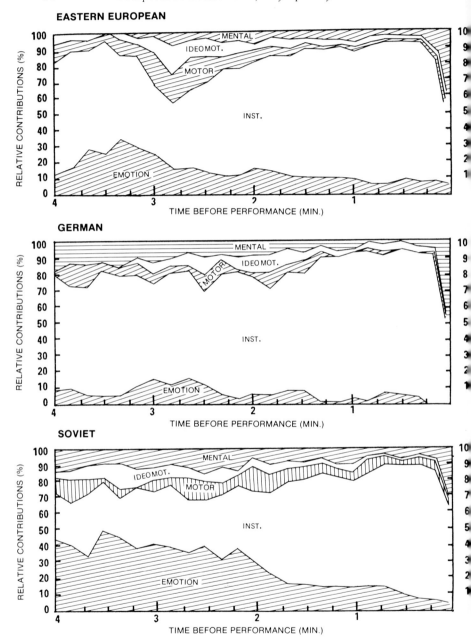

Figure 3-11.

types of specific equipment are required to be put on, adjusted, or taken off. Depending upon the event, long or short pants, hand guards or bare palms, suspension-type or support-type hand guards, rubber-soled or leather-soled slippers, and magnesium-covered or magnesium-free skin surfaces must be prepared prior to competing. All of these necessary, but demanding, acts must be meticulously executed in order that the gymnast have the material possibility of competing. These preparations are in addition to any motor, mental, or emotional management that is required in order to successfully accomplish the variety of tasks that confront the gymnast.

The magnitude of the frequency of these behaviors, when put into perspective with the varied physical and psychological demands of each event, demonstrates the importance of anticipating beforehand the great number of instrumental acts that must be performed. It is probable that not all gymnasts can and do anticipate these events, as was shown with Gienger in the introduction of this chapter, by efficiently getting them into a routine a long while ahead of time, so adequate physical and mental preparation time can still be accorded. It is a common experience to see gymnasts of an intermediate level inappropriately preparing for their material needs during the precious brief moments prior to competition, such as walking up to the event while buckling on their hand guards or putting on their suspenders. This means that they were not able to put their full concentration on the physical, psychological, or affective behaviors that could have been used to greater advantage than in the instrumental ones. As a general rule, it would seem best to get the material things out of the way in order to deal with the more subtle variables that concern performance.

The motor activities that take place during the brief four-minute period of preparation prior to competing occupy only about 6.7% of the Olympic gymnast's time. The very small portion of time that these physiological warm-up procedures take demonstrates that this dimension of performance, while being of high importance in sport science research (Franks, 1972; Neuberger, 1969), may in reality be of little importance at this stage of the competition process. The emphasis changes from a physiological to a psychological dimension in order to achieve successful performance. Since the nature of Olympic gymnastics is essentially anaerobic (Montpetit, 1976), it does not require that the gymnast be engaged in physiological or active motor preparation immediately prior to competing. Most of the preparation procedures of a physiological nature have taken place during the period of one to two hours prior to competing, at which time the essential strength and flexibility mechanisms mentioned in chapter 2 have been put into a state of readiness through appropriate warm-ups.

One example of how the Olympic gymnast is already physiologically prepared for competition during those last few moments is the Frenchman Henri Boerio, the bronze medal winner on the horizontal bar at Montreal. Henri, one of the most stylish of all the male gymnasts, would wait at ease on the bench among his teammates during their performances. Once the gymnast before him was finished competing, he shook off his jacket, chalked up, and jumped up on the apparatus. It was as if he had been waiting on the bench for his turn to work out during a practice session. While it may have been preferable to have systematically prepared himself mentally, as did Gienger earlier, one cannot argue with the possibility that there may be a wide range of acceptable preparatory procedures of a physiological nature, ranging from active preparation to doing nothing of a motor nature at all.

The ideomotor behaviors took up but 4.5% of all of the behaviors during this precompetitive phase. The fact that the motor or execution part of the preparation phase previously discussed was of the same approximate magnitude as were those procedures having an ideational or cognitive component points to the shift in the consideration of sport from purely a muscularly determined event to one also having an intellectual component. Kane (1978) has recently written about the cognitive components that are involved but usually not considered in the performance of most motor skills. During this precompetitive period it was observed that many gymnasts devoted at least a small portion of their time to the rehearsal of certain key movements in whole or in part. In some cases, it appeared that the gymnasts were rehearsing specific partial elements that were probably of importance to the overall success of the routine. For example, the eventual American bronze medal winner on the floor exercises, Peter Kormann, was repeatedly observed to be dynamically placing his arms and throwing them across his chest, as would occur in his double somersault with a full twist. After having performed this, he immediately rehearsed the safe landing position. Obviously, the setting of the twisting somersault and its successful landing were partial execution elements that Kormann believed were essential to his short-term preparation for this Olympic medal.

Other more frequent instances of ideomotor behaviors that were observed were those that involved the global execution of gymnastic routines. It was interesting that the men's and women's events that are generally considered to be the most difficult by the gymnasts, that is, the pommel horse and the balance beam, respectively, involved the most global ideomotor execution. It seems that even at this elite level, because of the high difficulty of maneuvers that the gymnasts are required to perform, along with the inherent risks of falling off certain apparatus, some degree of last-minute focusing of attention is necessary. The most evident ideomotor preparation was observed prior to the balance beam competition, at which time full routines on an imaginary beam could be rehearsed minutes before competing.

The preparation activities that were classed as being mental totalled 11% overall, sharing the second most important incidence of occurrence with the emotional behaviors. Again this points to the importance of cognitive components during the competition phase of high level athletics. Previously, Genov (1970) had observed the duration of the concentration periods immediately prior to Olympic weight lifting and found that the length of time increased with the amount of weight that was to be lifted. Given the complexity of the individual and combinations of elements that take place within one gymnastic routine, as well as the fact that either four or six completely different events are competed in, it could be proposed that the role of mental prestart preparation would be even more magnified in gymnastics than in weight lifting. The variety of routines to be performed on the different events in gymnastics would suggest that the brief moments prior to the moment of truth could be well spent in the mental rehearsal of their specific task demands. Nideffer (1976) suggests that, for such activities as gymnastics or diving, an internal narrowing of attention on the key elements that are essential for successful performance is needed. This would be in comparison to the type of broad internal focus for mental preparation that an athlete participating in a team activity such as football or ice hockey would undertake, since a wide number of varied alternative events would have to be reflectively considered.

It is instructive that the incidence of emotional activities occurring during his precompetitive phase is high (10.5%) as compared to the motor activities (6.7%). This emphasizes the point made by Salmela et al. (1979) that the muscular or other physiological systems are taxed in practice sessions while it is the nervous system that becomes the limiting factor in many competitions. Understandably, in a sport that requires so many quick and precise movements (Salmela, 1976), the management of stressful forces brought on by these demands, as well as by the additional situational pressures of an Olympic competition, could benefit from tension-reducing behaviors. One only has to consider the words of the great goaltender Jacques Plante of the Montreal Canadiens, when he reflected upon playing goal in a tension-packed situation, to appreciate why these gymnasts exhibited such a relatively high incidence of emotional behaviors. Plante proposed that the average office worker could only appreciate the potential tension that could arise in elite athletics if he or she were to imagine that there were 15,000 spectators watching his/her office work, and at each instance when an error was made, a red light went on and the spectators reacted by loud, collective verbal harassment. It is the need for protecting oneself against these potential types of destructive forces that causes the elite athlete to adopt these emotional or stress management strategies.

As was observed for the other pre– and postcompetitive behaviors, certain differences appeared in the preparatory behaviors of the male and female gymnasts observed at the Montreal Olympic Games. While the overall profiles of the behaviors of the men and women gymnasts that occurred prior to and after competing will be considered in chapter 7, certain elements can now be highlighted in this regard.

First, the only behavioral differences that were observed related to the ideomotor and emotional activities. The higher incidence of ideomotor behaviors for the female gymnasts was due to the fact that one of their four events, the balance beam, could be rehearsed integrally on a real or imaginary line on the floor, while the nature of men's events did not fully allow this possibility of ideomotor rehearsal. The absence of this modality of preparation by the men forced them to resort to purely mental preparation. While there was a greater tendency for mental preparation by the men (12.8%) than by the women (9.3%), these differences were not statistically significant.

However, the frequency of emotional behaviors observed for the females was significantly greater than that observed for the male gymnasts. This behavioral evidence that women demonstrate more emotionality than do men concurs with what was found during the postcompetitive affective reaction phase (see chapter 6). These behavioral patterns lend powerful support to the evidence found in personality tests (Kane, 1972) that shows that women are more emotional than men.

Again, it is only the emotional behavior patterns that differentiate the performance levels of the gymnasts, the other behavioral activities being similar, irrespective of the competency of the competitors. While Klavora (1975) states that there will be a reduction of anxiety with the increase in skill level, it appears that the highly charged situational factors for the highest scoring gymnasts in the 9.8 to 10.0 range are of such intensity that a greater level of emotional behaviors is induced at this level. It appears that the factors of the proximity of medals, the intensity of mass media coverage, and the physical presence of highly reputed athletes combine to cause a very emotionally tense situation in the highest competition performance bracket that does not occur when the gymnasts score less than 9.8 points. The visual image of the classic Soviet gymnast Ludmilla Tourischeva was very vivid during her preparation. Tourischeva continuously paced to and fro prior to competing, her mind totally focused upon her performance but her body moving without rest as she dispersed the nervous tension through this cathartic movement back and forth across the floor (see fig. 3-6). Whether it was due to age or to innate biological differences, Soviet world and Olympic champion

Nikolai Andrianov showed significantly fewer precompetitive nervous behaviors.

It was again only the behavioral category related to emotional activity that differentiated between the gymnasts of the various societies, the other states remaining similar in proportion. While the western European gymnasts showed a high incidence of emotional reactions to their performances and to their evaluation (see chapter 6), the degree of occurrence of emotional behaviors during this precompetitive phase was very low. This could indicate that the underlying processes of these two behaviors do not have a common psychological base. That is, the emotional state observed during the preparation phase might have been one of anxiety that was specifically related to the performance itself, while the reaction was purely an affective one related to the consequences of having finished, such as the magnitude of the mark or the relief of having finished. There was little correspondence between the pre– and postcompetitive affective states for the gymnasts from the societies that were extreme in their emotional behaviors. The Soviet gymnasts demonstrated the highest incidence of precompetitive emotional behaviors, while they were the least emotional in terms of the performance itself or its resultant score. Conversely the western European gymnasts showed the reverse pattern of emotional behaviors.

It may well be that gymnasts from one society have behavioral patterns that are as easily distinguishable while they are not competing as are their styles on the floor, which allow gymnastic experts to differentiate between Japanese and Russian techniques.

What does seem evident is that the Soviet gymnasts exhibited different behavior patterns from those gymnasts, such as the eastern Europeans, who are similar in sociocultural backgrounds or from those, such as the Japanese or German gymnasts, who are in similar competitive brackets. Some of the reasons for these differences in cultural behavioral patterns will be discussed further in chapter 8. Morton (1970) contends, however, that the rewards for international excellence for Soviet athletes is much greater than that of other societies. As one Soviet coach stated in an informal discussion, "You North Americans have the right to lose; for us, the consequences of losing are much greater."

POINTS OF INTEREST

• All gymnasts, regardless of sex, ability level, or society of origin, appear to prepare themselves similarly for competition in the manner that they warm up physically, rehearse mentally, or suit-up materially. Considering these behaviors, it can be said that "all gymnasts put on their pants one leg at a time."

• Emotional behaviors, however, show the most extreme and possibly the most functionally significant variations of all of the preparatory behaviors observed. This lends further support to the point of view that the psychological dimension is the most important and discriminating axis that separates the men from the women, the strongest performers from the weaker ones, and one society from another during this precompetitive preparatory phase.

• It is of note that when the gymnasts arrive in the upper echelon of the total field, then and only then do their emotional behavior levels change from those found at any of the lower levels. This increased pressure at the very top is one of which both gymnasts and coaches should be aware. Medals, or ultimate performance success, attract the most attention, and this level of competitive intensity causes performance breakdown or signs of stress that are not seen or experienced elsewhere.

• Gymnasts both of different sexes and from different societies showed emotional behaviors that varied a great deal. It was not clear, however, whether these differences were a result of innate biological differences; of varying socialization processes, values, or mores; or of the variation in the ages of the participating gymnasts.

• The behavior patterns that took place in the present observations of gymnastics may have been specific to individual sports in which the environment remains relatively stable. It may be that they would differ significantly for athletes preparing for individual activities in which the environment was unstable, such as fencing.

Chapter 4

SOCIAL STATES BEFORE COMPETITION

Two Hungarian Olympic gymnastics team members
wait together to compete.

Summary

In this chapter, the social states of the gymnasts during
the four-minute period prior to competing were classified

according to their type (alone, interaction, copresence) as well as to the role of the gymnasts' associates (teammates or coach). The most predominant social state was that of being alone. Depending upon the sex of the gymnast, the society of origin, and the length of time before competing, this state of being alone made up from 55% to 100% of all social states. The male gymnasts tended to spend more time in the presence of their teammates than did the females. The western European gymnasts spent the greatest amounts of time in the presence of either teammates or the coach, while the Soviets were alone 95% of the time. Specific social patterns were observed for the different societies.

THE OLYMPIC gymnast is in a fishbowl situation during the brief moments that he or she has to spend on the competition floor while performing complex routines before 15,000 spectators and five critical judges armed with rule books. However, prior to competing and immediately afterwards, these superb athletes are also observed, though less formally, by young fans (and behavioral observation researchers) in an attempt to empathize with how these athletes are dealing with these peak moments in their athletic careers.

One can imagine, depending upon the age, the sex, or even the country of origin of the gymnasts, that the social behaviors of these individuals might be widely different. These social behaviors concern how a particular gymnast relates to, or does not relate to, the coach or teammates. Without proposing intentions to these behaviors, it can be readily observed if a team is tightly knit, in the physical sense, by estimating the distance between the gymnasts and teammates or coaches. This quantitative measure can be evaluated in terms of whether an individual is in another individual's "personal space"—the imaginary capsule surrounding that person. Being within touching distance of another person is being within one's personal space and can be defined as being socially close.

However, being together physically can in some instances be accompanied by mental states that are universes apart, especially when both gymnasts are preparing in their own way for their performances and each is relating it to his/her own particular dreams, methods of preparation, and specific routine. In this case, the gymnasts can be said to be in a state of copresence, during which they are in close physical proximity and are working in parallel on their own task at hand. However, they can also be in close contact in a state of interaction, where they are talking or communicating nonverbally, perhaps to reassure one another either by a word of good luck or an arm on the shoulder.

Caution must be taken in trying to read intention into observed behaviors without having further complementary information, such as interviews of these athletes. For example, a gymnast preparing for competition alone in a corner may not reflect aloofness from his teammates but rather a true respect for the need for privacy of each gymnast preparing for competition in his own way. Conversely, being in close contact on a bench may reflect either a desire to be with one's colleagues, an order by the coach to stay together to help "team spirit," or a physical necessity because of lack of space.

In order to put the present observations on social states within a conceptual framework, the concepts of cohesion and rivalry must be considered. Cohesion between members of a team is often reported to be an essential ingredient for success in sport. Cohesion has been studied in sport psychology experimental and field studies and is usually experimentally defined as the result of all forces acting on members to remain in a group. However, attempts to relate cohesion positively with success in sport do not always come up with consistent results. The reason for the difficulty in establishing this relationship has been the variety of sport tasks studied as well as the many components that contribute to cohesion in a group.

In the present case, one measure of team cohesion could be the amount of social interaction between gymnasts, or even to their physical proximity to each other without verbal or nonverbal contact. However, as was pointed out earlier concerning intention, caution must be taken in reading too much into the observed behaviors, especially if one is attaching positive or negative qualities to these acts.

Rivalry during Olympic gymnastic competitions must also be considered when evaluating social states, since it is not limited just to athletes of other countries but includes one's own teammates. Within almost every team, there has occurred a lively battle in order to qualify for competition at this most prestigious event. Gymnastic powers such as Russia, Japan, and Rumania often divide the medals almost evenly between themselves, and this concentration of talent on a few teams increases the intensity of rivalry among members of a team of any one nation. This places these gymnasts in a paradoxical situation where they should attempt to be supportive of one another in order to help their country succeed for team placings and at the same time to withdraw and withhold support for teammates to allow themselves to do as well as possible.

Luschen (1970) has noted that a certain degree of rivalry among teammates, when balanced with team-building activities, can have an overall positive effect on the team results. The most appropriate combination of factors that will allow within-team rivalry to act as a stimulus to draw on unused resources to facilitate personal success is difficult to achieve. Too much team activity can bring everyone to a homogeneous level of mutual cooperation, but it may also destroy the winning edge of individual athletes that may be based upon idiosyncratic asocial behavior.

There is some evidence that the social behaviors of men and women in sport may differ. Alderman (1974) states that the differences in attitude between men and women in competition are probably not biological in nature but rather are results of differing mores, values, and taboos that they encounter in their socialization into sport. Bardwick (1971) points out that because women have traditionally not been socialized into sport in the same way as have men, they may demonstrate more subtle aggressive attitudes to rivals, such as the withdrawal of affectionate behaviors in competition.

Sherif (1976) indicates that in "feminine" sports, such as gymnastics or figure skating, the cloak of competition may be worn more easily by females, especially in the younger age brackets. Appearing to be too competitive is perceived as being a negative or masculine quality for a young woman in other types of competitive sport.

Fewer points of reference exist for the comparison of social states between societies. Morton (1970), in his treatise on sport in the Soviet Union, states, "Analysis of a nation at play reveals the stuff of its social fabric and value system, and tells us much about other facets of political and economic life, especially in modern society" (p. 13). Luschen (1970) also supports the position that the values and norms of a society may be shown in the profile of behaviors that its members exhibit. Further, Dickenson (1976) points out that these social behaviors might be less universal than are the functional preparatory behaviors for the execution of a task, since the former are more influenced by the various social contingencies and reinforcement patterns specific to each culture, while the latter become well-practiced stylized routines.

What must be avoided is the slotting in of social behaviors within established cultural stereotypes that have no factual basis. It is, however, more essential to accurately describe the selected social behaviors at this important moment in sport history so that this information can await its integration into social theory. One measure of the validity of these social states is the similarity of the present social behaviors and those occurring after the performance (see chapter 5).

In this chapter, the social states of the Olympic gymnasts during the four-minute precompetitive period were observed and compared between the male and female gymnasts and their society of origin.

RECORDING PROCEDURES

The present observations took place during the precompetitive period of four minutes or longer, during which the gymnasts readied themselves for the execution of their gymnastic routines. The space surrounding the competitive area was equipped with individual chairs upon which the gymnasts could sit, although they could sit apart from one another since there were approximately three chairs for each gymnast. The gymnasts also had an area of about 5 by 60 meters in which they could walk around or warm up. The observation was in some cases up to 10 minutes in length for some gymnasts. But in order to have a sufficient number of gymnasts, i.e. at least 85% of the cases, in the observation periods, all data were truncated at four minutes prior to competition. Observation of the preparatory functional behaviors (see chapter 3) were made concurrently with the social behaviors, since the latter did not change very frequently as compared to the former. The type of social behavior, its duration, and the associates in these behaviors were the variables of interest. Three types of social behaviors were operationally defined as being either alone, in a state of copresence, or in a state of interaction. The associates in the states of copresence and interaction could either be teammates or the coach. Thus, five possible social states could be observed in combining the type of behaviors and the type of associates involved.

Figure 4-1.   Nelli Kim of the Soviet Union paces to and fro away from any of her teammates or her coach.

The different behaviors were coded in terms of the observable verbal and/or gestural interactions between the gymnast in question and teammate(s) or coach(es). The state of being alone was operationally defined as being further than one arm's distance from anyone else (fig. 4-1). Copresence was defined as being within someone else's personal space of one arm's distance with no observed communication to be occurring between the individuals. Copresence could occur while the gymnasts were passively watching the competition, while warming up, or while doing any other preparatory activity (fig. 4-2). The state of interaction was defined as being any behaviors in which the gymnast talked, touched, rubbed, or smiled at another gymnast or coach (fig. 4-3). The duration of each social state was recorded in the manner outlined in chapter 1. The rate of consensus between the five observers for social states was 98.6% based upon samples every 15 seconds of the four-minute period for 88 parallel observations.

Figure 4.2.   Canadian gymnast Elfi Schlegel waits in copresence with her coach.

Figure 4-3. The West German coach interacts with the members of her team.

SEX

As can be seen in figure 4-4, the predominant social state during the four-minute period preceding the performance was that of being alone (79.5%), although no differences between the sexes were found with this variable. Differences were found, however, between sexes in terms of the relationship with the coach. Coaches were found to be to a greater extent in the presence of the females (3.7%) than they were with the male (1.2%) gymnasts (χ^2 (5) = 16.9, $p < .01$). The males, however, were observed to be in copresence (10.4%) as well as in interaction (3.7%) with their teammates more often than were the female (5.9% and 2.0%, respectively) gymnasts (χ^2 (9) = 34.4 and χ^2 (6) = 21.2, $p < .01$, respectively). No differences were found between the sexes in regards to interaction with the coach. Irrespective of the types of interactions, males spent more time with their teammates than did females (χ^2 (9) = 28.3, $p < .01$), while both spent similar amounts of time with the coach.

WOMEN

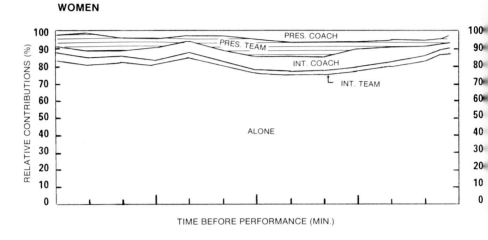

MEN

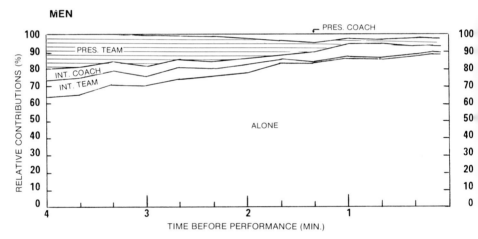

Figure 4-4. The relative contributions for the men and women of being alone, in interaction with teammates (int. team) or with the coach (int. coach), or in the copresence of a teammate (pres. team) or of the coach (pres. coach) are shown for the four minutes prior to competition. The men were more often with teammates, while the women spent more passive time with the coach.

SOCIETY

While being alone was the predominant social state, great variations occurred in its relative occurrence, as evidenced by that of the western Europeans (69.1%) in figure 4-5 and that of the Soviets (97.4%) in figure 4-6. No overall statistical differences, however, occurred for this variable, which averaged 79.5% across all societies. Overall, teammates spent about 7.9% of their time together in a state of copresence. Significant differences were found between societies on this dimension (χ^2 (5) = 13.31, $p <$ .05), with the western European teams remaining in close proximity to one another about 14.2% of the time while the Soviet gymnasts were only together for about .5% of the total four-minute duration. The state of copresence with the coach made up 4.8% of all social behaviors, and similarly to the other copresence patterns, the western Europeans were together with the coach the most (10.3% and the Soviet athletes (.5%) the least (χ^2 (5) = 12.4, $p <$ .05).

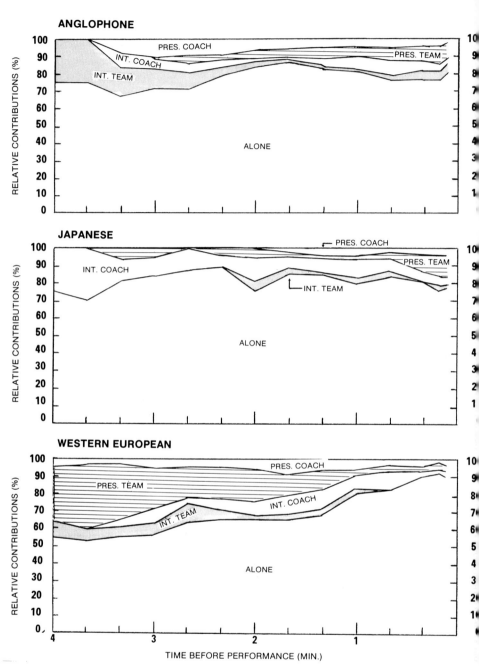

Figures 4-5 and 4-6. The western Europeans spent more time in the physical presence of their coaches and teammates while the Soviets spent the least. The Anglophones, Japanese, and Germans spent more time interacting with the coach, and the Soviets again were primarily alone.

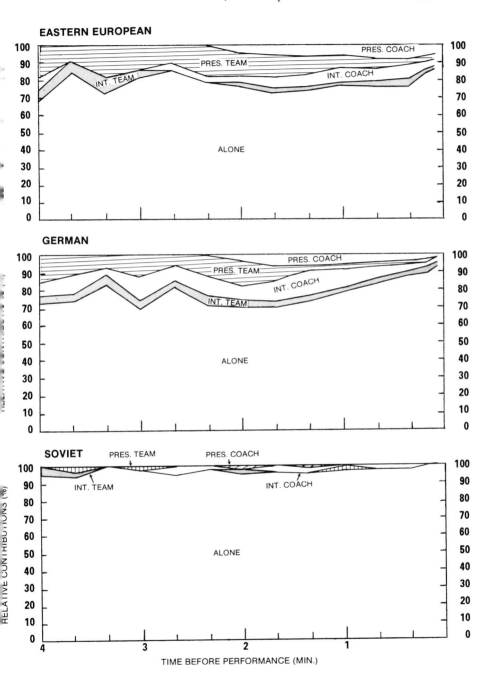

Figure 4-6.

Interaction between teammates contributed to only 3.16% of all social states, with significant differences occurring between societies (χ^2 (5) = 12.43, p < .05). The Anglophones had the greatest percentage of interactive behaviors (8.4%) with teammates, while the Soviets had the least interaction with fellow gymnasts (.5%). In terms of interaction with the coach, behaviors that contributed to 6.5% of all social states, differences were again found between societies (χ^2 (5) = 12.02, p < .05). The Japanese demonstrated the greatest incidence of interaction with the coach (12.2%), followed closely by the Germans (9.4%), while the Soviet gymnasts again showed the lowest occurrence of this behavior (.7%). When summed across all associates, the gymnasts were in an interactive state for about 9.7% of this four-minute period while being in copresence about 12.8% of the time. Conversely, the gymnasts spent about the same amounts of time with the coach (10.3%) and with teammates (10.5%), irrespective of the social state.

DISCUSSION

Considering the space restrictions in the competition arena, it was interesting to note that close to 80% of the gymnasts' last moments before competition were spent alone. Of course, this might be expected, given the nature of the sport task that was to be performed on any gymnastic event. The gymnast's performance at this level is highly overlearned, and during these last few minutes the key points in the routine are being dealt with by means of mental rehearsal, especially on those events such as balance beam and pommel horse, where a small error can be tragic. The type of short-term preparation necessary suggests that the athlete should adopt a narrow internal focus (Nideffer, 1976) on these key elements, rather than the broad external one that would be required to interact with teammates or the coach. This is even more evident when from about 40% to 95% of the preparatory behaviors during these last four minutes are instrumental in nature, such as putting on chalk and slippers or adjusting braces, hand guards, and leotards. Of all moments in the competition, these probably should be spent alone to assure the success of these meticulous adjustments.

Still, the fact that but 10.3% of all behaviors occur even near the coach may cause certain reflections on the role of the coach at these high level competitions once they are underway. It seems reasonable to assume that the role of the coach should be diminished once the gymnasts are ready to perform as compared to during the learning phases in practice sessions. In a similar manner, it was found that the feedback of a correctional nature that these same gymnasts received (see chapter 6) was very minimal as compared to that occurred at practice in other sports (Brunelle et al., 1978; Tharp & Gallimore, 1976). This should be a warning for the novice coach in competitions to diminish the tendencies to "overcoach" that are developed in practice. Rather, the new role should be one of highlighting briefly key points and making sure that all technical details, such as adjusting equipment and knowing the order of competition, are anticipated and carried out without the gymnast's awareness. The coach should be like a good restaurant waiter. The gymnast knows that a good job was done if the coach was not seen, but someone was being attentive to all that did and could happen.

One small incident was observed that illustrates the invisibility of the coach that is necessary for the efficient functioning of the team in Olympic competition. In that the warm-up period is but three minutes per team before each event, time is at a premium. Prior to each event, the young female West German coach ran ahead to the next apparatus to check mats, adjust the bars, or dust off the beam. The honor of marching in close social contact with the team to the acknowledgment of the appreciative crowd was bypassed for the efficient warm-up of her charges.

Figure 4-7. The West German coach prepares the balance beam before the arrival of her team. An example of efficiency in coaching.

Despite the necessity of remaining apart from the gymnast in these important final minutes to allow the fullest concentration and preparation to occur, a case can still be made for the role of the coach as a strong psychologically supportive person during that period by means of some small significant act. In very broad terms it can be said that the muscular system is stressed in practice while the nervous system is the limiting factor in competition. Thus, a reassuring word or a pat on the buttock (modern coaching's psychological answer to the aspirin) can let the gymnast know that positive support will be received irrespective of the

result of the performance. This moment of truth must be anticipated by the coach and approached in a calm manner; otherwise,
any anxieties the coach manifests will be transmitted to the
gymnast in an already tense situation. The coach should be able
to evaluate his/her own behaviors in competition to remedy any
such anxiety-producing situations that are caused by him/her and
not just by the competition.

Comparisons of the social behaviors between the men and the
women gymnasts revealed overall patterns of being alone that, at
first glance, were remarkably similar. However, as was stated
earlier (chapter 2), a great deal of instrumental behavior, such as
adjusting their uniforms, took place during that period. Dickenson (1976) points out that such functional behaviors would be
relatively immune to sexual or cultural differences, while the
social behaviors would be more influenced by these factors.

The greatest differences between the male and female social
behaviors concerned the amount of time spent with teammates.
The males spent significantly more time with their associates than
did the females. One interpretation of this finding is the argument of Bardwick (1971) regarding women in competitive situations withholding reward, in this case personal presence, as a
subtle aggressive behavior reflecting their unassuredness in the
competitive sport world. Some anecdotal support for this viewpoint has been volunteered by coaches who have worked with
both men and women. For whatever reason, they report that the
men are looser in terms of relating to one another, while the
women can be quite sharp during these moments of stress.

Probably, one important determining factor for these differences between sexes is that of age. As was mentioned in chapter
2, the average age of the 103 male gymnasts in Montreal was 23.4
years, while the 100 females averaged 18.0 years. Assuming that
both groups began training at about the same age, the male
gymnasts would have had about five extra years of competition
during which the activity might have been put in a better life
perspective in terms of the competition and the role of teammates
in that drama. For the above reason, it is possible that the females
were in greater contact with their coach, since they had not yet
developed the independence that might come with age.

It is important to note that the overall profiles of the two sexes in these precompetitive social states were comparable to the post-competitive feedback patterns (see chapter 6) . In both cases, the males received more social attention from teammates, and there was a large percentage of routines where the gymnast received no social support before or after competition.

The greatest differences in the profiles of the social states occurred when comparisons were made between the society of origin of the gymnasts. For whatever reasons, the profiles of the Soviet gymnasts were very different from those of all other societies, with less than 5% of their behaviors being executed in conjunction either with the coach or teammates. Interpretation of these differences is, however, a more difficult task. One is reminded that there are inherent dangers in the interpretation of national stereotypes and national character in psychological research. Lippman (1953) points out that, ". . . for the most part, we do not see and then define, we define first and then see. In the great blooming, buzzing confusion of the outer world we pick out what our culture has already defined for us and we tend to perceive that which we have picked out in the form stereotyped for us by our culture" (p. 244) .

Nevertheless, some cautious interpretations can be attempted to explain this extreme profile. First of all, it is difficult to attribute these differences to a political regime, since the eastern European countries share the same governmental systems to some degree. In fact, the eastern Europeans' social behavioral profiles strikingly resemble those of the two Germanies. The argument that these differences are the result of skill level, with the Soviets demonstrating profiles that are compatible with excellence, also does not receive support. The majority of the Japanese observations were made on the winning men's team, and their profile of social states was very different from that of the Soviets.

One interpretation from a Soviet viewpoint is offered by Hanin (1977) , who states that these social behaviors are specifically learned in training, enabling the gymnast to withdraw into his/her own personal space capsule and concentrate on the task at hand. In all probability, the reason for this extreme profile is more likely a combination of these preparatory techniques with cultural values that emphasized the importance of winning at the risk of not appearing sociable. This latter interpretation is judged as being valid, since the Soviets also demonstrated similar consistently extreme patterns in the postperformance social feedback profiles. Finally, the overall excellence of both the men and women Soviet gymnasts would probably cause greater rivalry in the search for individual medals than is the case within other teams.

In comparison, the western European and the Anglophone gymnasts demonstrated the greatest levels of social interaction. It is possible to hypothesize that more social behaviors could be exhibited between these gymnasts since they were not as likely to be battling for the medals. However, this large percentage of time spent together should not be interpreted as a measure of cohesion, unless the cohesion as measured by "togetherness" was one that was externally imposed. For example, the American women always marched in step together and sat side by side on the team bench. This discipline does not necessarily mean that cohesion, as measured by other means (Carron, 1977), was a reality.

A special comment is reserved for the profile of the Japanese team, which showed a very high incidence of interaction between the gymnasts and the coach. On a personal visit to Japan, it was noted that the coach played a very passive role in practice and that the gymnasts imposed their own discipline in workouts by themselves. Often the coach stayed in his office or on a balcony during training. In competition, the coach was the last to send off the gymnast with a pat and the first to greet him after the routine with a handshake in a paternalistic manner. When the great gymnast Tzukahara was questioned on the apparent joy that the men Japanese gymnasts demonstrated in competition as compared to other nations, he replied, "We cry in practice, we laugh in competition."

The coherence displayed in these patterns of social behavior with those occurring during the postcompetitive feedback phase (see chapter 6) between both sexes and societies hints at a common, if yet undetected, cause or causes behind these fascinating sport scenarios.

POINTS OF INTEREST

• The social constellations of the gymnasts and their teammates and coaches may provide means of evaluating or elaborating upon such concepts as team spirit, cohesion, rivalry, and the coaching behaviors during this period.

• The predominant social state of the elite competitive gymnast is one of being alone. It is essential that the gymnast become completely self-reliant during these last minutes of mental and physical preparations in the form of covert and overt rehearsal, stress management, and energy mobilization for the upcoming routine. Most of these preparations had to be accomplished in the same state as that of the performance—by oneself.

• The role of active "coaching," conversely, is one that must now be reconsidered. The active counselling, correcting, and sanctioning that takes place during practice sessions must be replaced by quiet support and pats on the bottom.

• The concept of team cohesion may be of less direct consequence in an individual sport such as gymnastics; however, the strong supportive force of caring teammates may have long-range effects that go beyond the brief competitive moments.

• In contrast, if physical distance can be interpreted as measure of team rivalry, it may be that this may act as a positive stimulus for performance, although long-range benefits on a human level are questionable.

Chapter 5

IMMEDIATE PERFORMANCE FEEDBACK*

Kurt Thomas of the United States is congratulated
by his coach.

*Portions of text from the *Journal of Human Movement Studies,* 5:77-84, 1979,
Lepus Books, London. Reprinted with permission of the publisher.

Summary

In this chapter, the feedback patterns received upon dismounting from the apparatus were classified in terms of their type (positive, negative, information, or no feedback) as well as their source (coach, teammates, or multiple sources). The most frequent type of feedback received was positive in nature, followed closely by "no feedback." The coach was the most frequent source of this positive information. Women tended to receive more feedback from their coaches, while men received more from teammates. Feedback was contingent upon the performance result both in kind and amount. Gross differences were observed between the feedback patterns across the six societies studied.

THE GYMNAST executes intricate movement patterns that tax not only the physical but also the perceptual systems, both in time and space (Salmela, 1976). The body then alights effortlessly, performing the dismount without wavering. The resolution of this complex perceptual-motor problem with apparent ease has taken years of practice, which allows the gymnast to precisely evaluate the completed performance by means of movement-produced feedback. It is, however, clear that this same moment, when occurring during an Olympic performance, will be forever crystallized along with the immediate consequences of the performance success or failure. The feedback that is received from associates or mentors, whether it be in the form of information or sanction, could provide an external validation of the perceptions arising from internal sources. The observation of the patterns of this postperformance feedback is the subject of the present chapter.

The broad concept of feedback has enjoyed a central position in current psychological thought, ranging from the neuropsychological research of fine-grain movement control circuitry to large-scale behavior management programs (Rushall & Siedentop, 1972). In this chapter, a line of thought will be developed from the traditional experimental research to current behavioral investigations on feedback in sport situations. A position that is situated on the far end of the continuum of methodologies from experimental to behavioral research on feedback will be undertaken.

In their classic work, Bilodeau and Bilodeau (1961) stated that, "Studies of feedback or knowledge of results . . . show it to be the strongest, most important variable controlling performance and learning" (p. 250). Using discrete movement reproduction tasks, information feedback (IF) was defined as being only those stimuli under the control of the experimenter that were related to the subject's response. More recently, Deci (1975) has attempted to elaborate a cognitive approach to intrinsic motivation by integrating within the concept of reward the components of sanction, i.e. praise or criticism, with the component of IF, i.e. performance feedback.

The sanctioning dimension is related to the positive or negative value of the behavior, in contrast to IF, which is concerned with the magnitude of the response error. It was found that the motivational effect of both the sanction and information components was perceived differently, depending on whether the subjects were male or female. In addition to these sexual differences, Maehr (1974) has also shown that Americans and Iranians did not perceive rewards in the same manner. It therefore appears that the concept of feedback might well be studied in consideration of the independent variables of sexual and cultural dimensions.

More recently, the nature of feedback given to young athletes in a learning situation, along with other teaching behaviors, have been evaluated using behavioral assessment techniques. Brunelle, Talbot, Tousignant, Hubert and Ouellet (1978) evaluated the type of performance feedback hockey instructors gave young boys from 9 to 11 years of age during sessions in hockey schools. Of the 4800 teaching behaviors reported, 48.9% were related to the evaluation of the performance either through sanction or IF. This information was for the most part IF (68.4%), relating to the correction of performance techniques, while the balance (31.6%) was made up of positive or negative sanctions of the player's behavior. Positive feedback was observed four times more frequently than negative feedback. In a study of the behaviors of Little League baseball coaches, Smoll, Smith and Hunt (1977) reported that interviewed Little League players interpreted the absence of feedback from coaches as being a negative sanction of their performance. Orlick (1978) supported this need for feedback from coaches as being one of the determining factors that caused young children to remain in or to drop out of minor league hockey programs.

Finally, in a case study of a successful American college basketball coach, Tharp and Gallimore (1976) found a relatively high percentage of verbal (50.3%) and nonverbal (4.4%) IF regarding ". . . what to do and how to do it." Feedback giving positive and negative sanctions totaled 14.7% of all observed behavior, with praise having the greatest contribution (6.9%) as compared to scolding (6.6%) and nonverbal positive feedback (1.2%). A substantial contribution of scolding followed by IF (8.0%) was observed in the 2326 observed acts of teaching. The greater emphasis on negative feedback in the latter study as compared to the study by Brunelle and associates (1978) was probably due to the age and maturity of the athletes. That is, older athletes were better prepared to handle scolding than younger ones. The performance consequences of training for a national championship were also greater than the more informal learning occurring at a hockey school.

While behavioral data do exist on feedback patterns during the learning and training of athletes of different ages, similar patterns of feedback are not available on high level performers during elite competition. Presumably, feedback at this level would have both a sanctioning and an informational role for the athlete in terms of performance, although the emphasis would be different than that in a training situation. However, prior to the attempted explanation of the role of IF or rewards, a description of the phenomenon is necessary. Observation of feedback patterns following elite performance in a natural setting would be instructive, especially when highlighted across the previously determined salient dimensions of the subjects' sex (Deci, 1975), cultural origin (Maehr, 1974), and level of ability (Brunelle et al., 1978; Smoll et al., 1977).

RECORDING PROCEDURES

The present observations took place during the postperformance period that began when the gymnast descended from the competition platform and returned to the assigned team bench. The limited space surrounding the competitive platform provided ample opportunity for the gymnast to encounter coaches, teammates, accompanying personnel (i.e. pianist, assistant coaches, managers), as well as gymnasts from other teams. This period of observation lasted approximately 15 seconds. The type of feedback received as well as the source of the feedback were the variables of interest. Based upon the observed operationally defined behaviors, the types of feedback were classed as being either a "positive" or "negative" sanction of the performance. Behaviors judged to convey technical points on the performance through verbal or nonverbal means were classified as being "information feedback." The absence of the above behaviors was termed "no feedback." While more than one type of feedback could be given (Tharp & Gallimore, 1976), no instances were observed. The sources of the feedback were the coach only, the team only, the coach and the team, the team and accompanying personnel, and adversaries. As outlined in the tenets of applied behavior analysis (Baer, Wolf, & Rislcy, 1968), intention cannot readily be observed,

Figure 5-1. An East German gymnast gives positive feedback to a gymnast from the Soviet Union after her successful routine.

only its behavioral manifestations. What is essential is precise operational definitions through behavior coding and reliable observation.

Coding of the various types and sources of feedback was based upon observable verbal and/or nonverbal interactions between the returning gymnast and the coaches, gymnasts, and others in the immediate competitive area. While it cannot be said that feedback was actually transmitted, either in terms of reward or information, by the observation of behavior, the operationally defined behaviors can be used as inferential criteria that feedback had taken place. Positive feedback was defined as being those verbal or nonverbal behaviors of the individuals in the immediate vicinity of the gymnast that reflected a positive sanction of the just-completed performance. These behaviors included hand shaking, patting on the shoulder or buttocks, hugging or kissing of the gymnast, leaning towards the gymnast while making a remark with a smile or a wink, or by establishing "eye contact" and nodding, winking, or smiling. Some acknowledgment of this feedback by means of perceivable orientations towards its source was observed but was not necessary in order that this behavior be recorded.

Negative feedback was defined as being those verbal or nonverbal behaviors reflecting negative sanction of the performance by individuals in the immediately surrounding area during this postcompetitive period. These behaviors included frowning, shaking the head from side to side, slapping the hands or kicking the feet in disgust, turning away, or curtly remarking something to the gymnast with a stern face, all the while maintaining "eye contact" with the gymnast.

A "no feedback" situation was that in which the gymnast was not acknowledged at all by the coach, teammates, or other individuals in the immediate area. No observable communication occurred between the gymnast and associates; rather, the gymnast returned to the bench and sat down or got dressed and did not receive any verbal or nonverbal contact from those people in the surrounding areas.

Information feedback was defined as being those nonemotional observed behaviors that took place between the gymnasts and team-

Figure 5-2. A Canadian coach gives information feedback on a technical point to a gymnast after his routine.

mates or coaches and were characterized by extended verbal explanations and/or gestures, presumably concerning a substantive matter of gymnastic technique. The facial expression of the individuals giving the feedback was demonstrating neither positive (smiling) nor negative (frowning) sanction but was judged to be concerned. Gesticulations representing gymnastic movement patterns were in themselves sufficient to be classified as carrying technical information, even when not accompanied by verbal explanation.

Applause from the spectators was not considered to be feedback, since it occurred for all performances without exception.

Overall Feedback Patterns

The overall frequencies of the different types of observed feedback as well as the sources are indicated in table 5-I. It can be seen that behaviors interpreted to represent positive feedback occurred in 441 cases, or in 61.8% of the total 714 observations. The coach alone accounted for the greatest single source of feedback (38.1%), followed by the coach and the team together (15.4%), and finally by members of the team only (8.2%). In the subsequent analyses, all feedback from sources other than only from the team or only from the coach are pooled into a single class termed "multiple sources" in order to have sufficient

Figure 5-3.   Ludmilla Tourischeva receives no feedback on her balance beam
routine from Olga Korbut of the Soviet Union.   (With permission from J.H.
Salmela, *Journal of Human Movement Studies,* 1979, 5, 77–84) .

observations for analysis.   No instances of negative feedback were
reported in any of the observations in the analysis.   Behaviors

TABLE 5-I

OVERALL OBSERVED FREQUENCIES OF THE SOURCE
AND TYPE OF FEEDBACK RECEIVED
FOLLOWING OLYMPIC GYMNASTIC PERFORMANCE

	Feedback Type[a]	
Source	Positive[b]	Information
Coach only	236 (33.1)	36 (5.0)
Coach and Team	56 (7.8)	3 (0.4)
Team only	110 (15.4)	0 (0)
Team and Others	26 (3.6)	0 (0)
Others[c]	13 1.8)	0 (0)

Note: No feedback was received in 234 cases (33.4%) .
[a] No instances of negative feedback were observed.
[b]Numbers in parentheses indicate the relative contributions in percentage
of each behavior.
[c] Refers to officials and/or acompanying personnel.

considered to be conveying information feedback were observed in a total of 5.5% of the total sample, with the very large majority coming from the coach. A large percentage (32.8%) of the observed behaviors indicated that no feedback of any sort was communicated to the gymnast.

SEX

The observed feedback patterns for both male and female gymnasts are presented in figure 5-4. A chi square for independence of samples showed that the overall feedback patterns of the two sexes were significantly different (χ^2 (4) = 44.88, $p < .001$), with each feedback category contributing substantially to the overall result. In terms of frequency of response, positive feedback from the coach and no feedback occurred most often for both sexes. The men received more positive feedback from the team and from multiple sources, while the women received more positive feedback from the coach, more information feedback, and a greater instance of no feedback.

PERFORMANCE LEVEL

The observed patterns of feedback compared across levels of performance are shown in figure 5-5. Statistical analysis reveals that the patterns of feedback are not independent of the performance level (χ^2 (16) = 43.44, $p < .001$). Individual comparisons between performance levels revealed that all groups differed from one another at the .05 level of confidence except the fourth highest score bracket from the second and third levels, respectively. The incidence of positive feedback from the coach differed from the next most frequent category, no feedback (χ^2 (4) = 16.63, $p < .01$). This difference, however, resulted mainly from the comparatively low level of positive feedback from the coach for the poorest performers and from the relatively low level of no feedback for the best performers. Positive feedback only from the team tended to decrease as the performances became better. In general, the extreme performance levels received atypical feedback patterns as compared to the middle groups. In a tertiary analysis, the total positive feedback increased in importance as the competition advanced from the compulsory exercises (55.1%) to

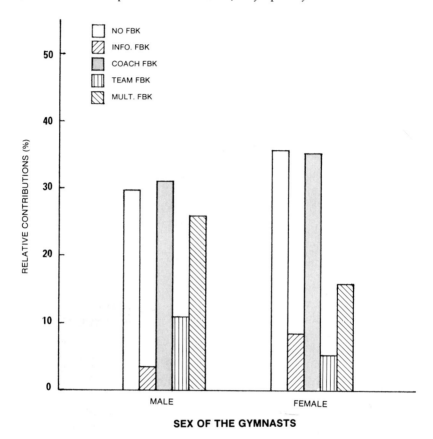

Figure 5-4.   The relative contributions of no feedback (no fbk), information feedback (info. fbk), and positive feedback from the coach (coach fbk), the team (team fbk), or from multiple sources (mult. fbk) are shown for male and female gymnasts.   Males received more positive feedback from teammates and multiple sources, while females received more positive and information feedback from the coach and more instances of no feedback.

the optionals (64.0%) and even more substantially in the finals (76.9%). It was of further interest that information feedback was observed with the greatest relative frequency during the finals (17.0%).

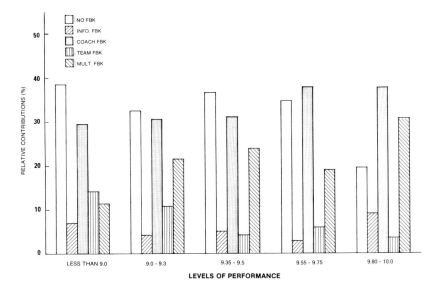

Figure 5-5. The feedback patterns for the different performance levels show a general increase in positive feedback from the coach and multiple sources and a decrease in no feedback as gymnasts' performance levels increase.

SOCIETY

The distributions of the observed feedback patterns as a function of the society of the participating gymnasts are presented in figure 5-6. The overall statistical analysis reveals that the feedback patterns are not independent of the society of origin of the participating gymnasts (χ^2 (20) $= 134.88$, $p < .001$). Comparison of any two groups shows that no two feedback patterns are alike. However, the Anglophone, Japanese, and Germanic gymnasts had the most similar feedback patterns. Greatest variations in any one feedback type were observed in the no feedback category, with the Japanese having the lowest occurrence and the eastern Europeans the highest of this type. Information feedback was never observed to be given to the Japanese gymnasts, while both eastern and western European gymnasts received the most. The Germanic and Japanese gymnasts received the greatest relative proportions of positive feedback from the coach, while the lowest contribution of this type of feedback came from the Soviet, eastern European, and western European coaches, respectively. When all sources of positive feedback were totalled, the Japanese gymnasts received the greatest proportion (83.1%), followed by the Germans (80.3%), the Anglophones (77.2%), the western Europeans (56.9%), the Soviets (46.9%), and finally the eastern Europeans (43.7%).

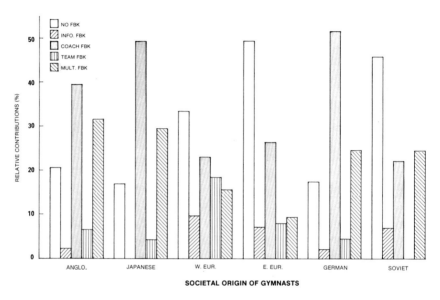

Figure 5-6. Extremely varied feedback patterns are shown between the gymnasts of different societies. Most striking are the high levels of positive feedback from the German and the Japanese coaches and the high levels of no feedback from the Soviet and eastern European gymnasts.

DISCUSSION

The assessment of the feedback patterns for Olympic gymnasts, as evidenced in the present study, provides a bank of behavioral data that, with few exceptions (Brunelle et al., 1978; Smoll et al., 1974; Tharp & Gallimore, 1976), is nonexistent in the study of sport. This type of procedure can be situated methodologically somewhere between natural ethological observation and applied behavior analysis. In that the predetermined behaviors were coded by trained observers in this specific situation, the present study could be likened to the initial baseline phase of applied behavior analysis, without the addition of the experimental conditions that normally follow. However, the fact that cultural, sexual, and skill level comparisons were possible by regrouping the independent variables, a broad anthropological portrait of these postperformance variables results.

Prerequisite to the behavioral assessment of any phenomenon is the demonstration that the percent of agreement between two observers' coding of the phenomenon is within acceptable limits. It is worth noting that, while within an acceptable range, the greatest cause of disagreement occurred between the categories of information feedback and positive feedback from the coach. This differentiation between praise and information, the two components of reward or feedback, might be as difficult for an external observer to make as it is for the receiver to perceive in the intrinsic motivation research (Deci, 1975).

The overall feedback patterns observed when the data are in their ungrouped form (see table 5-I) differ somewhat from other reported behavioral observations. In the present study, no instances of negative feedback were observed, while Brunelle et al. (1978) found some instances (3.09%) of scolding remarks from hockey instructors with 9– to 12-year-old boys. Tharp and Gallimore (1976) observed that over 14% of all social reinforcements, either verbal or nonverbal, given to a top caliber American college basketball team were negative in nature, as compared to less than 7% positive feedback. It should be pointed out that the above studies occurred during learning sessions occurring in closed or private environments, where negative feedback might be appropriate.

The lack of negative sanctions found in this study was probably due to the fact that there would be little functional value in criticizing in such a setting since the performance would not be repeated. However, positive feedback and IF would be useful means of maintaining the appropriate psychological state for competition. Further, the high level of automatization of gymnastic routines at the Olympic level would rarely provide sufficient warrant for overt negative sanctions usually associated with tactical errors or lack of effort in interactive sports such as hockey and basketball. It is quite probable that negative sanctions might have been intended by the coaches, and perceived by the gymnasts, in the large percentage of cases when no feedback was given at all (31.4%). Smoll et al. (1977) interviewed Little League players about their interpretations of the coach's reactions to their performance. In many cases, no feedback was believed to be equivalent to negative feedback. It could be suggested that the fairly high level of no feedback might be interpreted in this manner and that the gymnast may come "down to the ground," both literally and figuratively, after the performance.

The overwhelming type of feedback observed in this study was of the positive variety, totaling 63.1% of all behaviors. The discrete nature of the routines, as well as the scarcity of unexpected errors, would cause these concentrations of positive feedback to be predictably higher than the previously mentioned behavioral assessments of feedback. The present observations demonstrate that the gymnasts receive a substantial portion of their postperformance feedback (20.5%) from sources other than the coach, i.e. the team only, the team and others, other associate personnel only, and/or adversaries. In contrast to the data of Brunelle et al. (16.02%) and Tharp and Gallimore (50.3%), a low percentage of information feedback in the present study (5.5%) was observed. Again, the routinized performance of a well-learned sequence in a gymnastic event as compared to the learning of new motor skills would explain these differences.

While the type of feedback received is important, it may be that the timing of this feedback at the most critical moment is even more essential. For example, negative or information feedback probably does not serve a useful purpose when given immediately after an unsuccessful performance, with the exception of possibly making the coach feel better. The gymnast knows better than anyone else what has gone wrong. Additional information of a negative or technical nature might only disrupt the upcoming routines that lay ahead. In the situation of a missed routine, it would probably be more appropriate to hold off negative comments altogether and to delay more technical ones for a quiet moment after the competition. Again, positive feedback would be inappropriate in this case, if directed to the performance outcome ("nice routine"), but it might be supportive if it was intended for the effort of the gymnast on a difficult event ("good try, now settle down for the next event").

When regrouped according to the sex of the gymnasts, the feedback types showed different patterns for the men and the women. The women tended to get more feedback from the coach and less feedback from their teammates, while the reverse was shown true for the men. The rules for this competion stated that the coach on the floor must be the same sex as the gymnasts. It could be offered that the women gymnasts show different aggressive behaviors when compared to the men because of different patterns of socialization in sport. Bardwick (1971) pointed out that this could result in women demonstrating subtle aggressive actions in competition, such as the withdrawal of feedback from teammates. The men, however, could act out their aggression more overtly and thus demonstrate more camaraderie with their teammates. In that high level competition has, until recently, been less socially acceptable for women than for men, it is possible that the female coach may wish to overcompensate and to reassure the gymnasts more than would the male coach. This may also explain why the women received more than twice the information feedback as the men. Feedback patterns for men and women gymnasts in practice situations would be of interest.

These differential feedback patterns between the sexes might eventually find explanation in terms of intrinsic motivation concepts (Deci, 1977). Recent data in this area show that females tend to persist less when an extrinsic reward is attached to the outcome. On the contrary, males have been shown to demonstrate greater intrinsic motivation, as evidenced by greater persistence, when an extrinsic reward was included for performance. Differentially appropriate feedback patterns may be desirable if the intent is to maintain a gymnasts' interest and keep him/her in the sport. Behavioral differences between the sexes were also observed for the variables of interest during the precompetitive period (Hallé, 1978; Salmela, 1978).

Part of the differences that occur between the sexes in the respective feedback received can be attributed to the varied requirements of the 10 gymnastic events from a psychomotor point of view (Salmela, 1976a). The perceived difficulty of the event can elicit differential emotional reactions from teammates or coaches. For example, both men's and women's vault resulted in lowest levels of positive feedback, while balance beam and rings received the highest praise. These events could be interpreted in attribution theory terms (Weiner, 1974), by which activities that are perceived as requiring certain elements of luck (the vault landing) receive lower causal attributions than those requiring skill or effort (balance beam control and ring effort). Direct evaluation by interviews of the perceived difficulty of the different events would provide means of verifying these hypotheses.

The level of performance of the competing gymnast seems to be related to the type of feedback that was received. It appears that only in the highest performance bracket was the incidence of no feedback substantially different than that observed for any of the lower score levels. It was also somewhat paradoxical that the greatest incidence of information feedback regarding technical matters occurred at this highest level, followed closely by the observed information feedback in the lowest performance bracket. Competitive aggressiveness or envy between gymnasts may be evidenced by the fact that teammates accorded less positive feedback with increasing scores. The reflected glory for a winning coach may explain the observed increase in conveying positive feedback to the gymnasts as the performance scores increased.

As the importance of the competition progressed from the preliminaries to the finals, a general increase in the total positive feedback given was noted. It is evident that the rewards of social reinforcement are contingent upon the results of the performance. The high incidence of information feedback in the event finals is somewhat perplexing, since this technical information could in no way help performances at that competition, as might have been the case if this information was given earlier during the preliminaries. The demonstration by the coach to the many spectators in this "fishbowl situation" that he or she does possess observable coaching skills may be the reason for the demonstration of these behaviors, rather than the intent of informing the gymnast of a technical point.

The final regrouping of these feedback patterns was done as a function of the nationalities of the competing gymnasts. It would appear quite clear from the extreme variations in the feedback patterns that there was a cultural influence that determined how and by whom feedback is given. Maehr (1974) suggested that cultural differences in achievement motivation necessitated that an ethnographic approach to such problems be undertaken to broaden the base of theoretical experimentation. In the present ethnographic comparisons, certain communalities and differences leap from data. The levels of the no feedback category for both the eastern European countries (49.1%) and the Soviet Union (45.9%) were extremely high as compared to the lower levels for the Japanese (16.9%) and Germanic (17.5%) societies. The two socialist societies also demonstrated relatively lower levels of total positive feedback as compared to the highest levels observed with the Japanese. In general terms, the Anglophone, Japanese, and Germanic profiles resembled each other in proportion, as did the eastern European countries and the Soviet Union. The Soviet gymnasts also showed behavior patterns for social states, preparatory behaviors and emotional reactions that differed from other societies even when equated by political grouping as well as performance level (Salmela, 1977). The western European countries had an overall profile that was intermediate to the former two groups but resembling to a greater extent the profiles for the socialist countries.

POINTS OF INTEREST

• Feedback to gymnasts received immediately after they have performed appears to be very different from that received in practice. In competition, no negative and very little information feedback is given, while in practice the reverse is true. Higher levels of positive feedback were observed in this competitive situation than were observed in other practice situations, although this is not necessarily a desirable tendency.

• One third of all performances were followed by no feedback at all. It could be argued that no feedback was necessary at that moment, since the most important learning feedback has already been given during the learning phase of practice. However, an optimal performance state might be better maintained if gymnasts were in some small way acknowledged after having completed their routine.

- The frequency of feedback of a positive sort seemed to be directly related to the absolute performance level of the gymnast. The gymnasts whose scores were high received greater amounts of positive approval from peers. Gymnasts at the lower levels, while also possibly performing to their full capacity, received less attention from their teammates and coaches. These psychological rewards appear to be distributed based upon absolute performance rather than relative progress.

- The greatest source of positive feedback is the coach, not the teammates. Within the whole competitive process that takes place within this brief five-minute period, this may be the most effective moment for any type of "coaching" intervention.

- The most appropriate feedback after a missed performance in gymnastics is difficult to prescribe. Is technical information of use at this moment, or should the gymnast be consoled positively? It may be best for the coach to show his/her support, either verbally or nonverbally, and then leave the gymnast alone for a while in order to remobilize his/her composure for the next event.

Chapter 6

EMOTIONAL REACTIONS UPON DISMOUNTING

Nadia Comaneci reacts happily to her perfect 10 score.

Summary

In this chapter, a classification was made of the observable emotional or affective reactions of the gymnasts immediately following their performance and its evaluation. Both reactions to the performance and to the evaluation

99

were operationally defined as being positive, negative, or
without emotional response. Higher frequencies of affective
reactions were observed for the performance as compared to
its evaluation. Positive reactions were observed more frequently than negative ones; however, the behavior "no
response" was predominant. Different profiles of observed
emotional responses were recorded for the male and female
gymnasts, with the females showing more positive and negative emotional behaviors. The incidence of positive emotional responses increased with higher scores. Extreme
variation was observed in the positive emotional reaction of
the gymnasts from the Soviet Union, western Europe, and
the Anglophone countries.

WHO CAN forget those images emanating from the Montreal
Forum and transmitted across the world in July 1976? A
full young Soviet gymnast with slightly Oriental features named
Nelli Kim came hurtling over the vaulting horse while double
somersaulting in one axis and twisting 360 degrees in the other to
end in a perfect stand. An immediate smile broke across her
pretty face, endearing her to the world. Seconds later, the perfect
score of 10 is flashed, and again that radiant smile. While gymnastic aficionados will remember the perfection of the full twisting Tzukahara vault, millions more will retain that unforgettable
human emotional reaction.

The affective reaction to this previously unseen women's vault
by Kim was understandable, since a landing such as hers, in which
her feet seemed stuck in glue, immediately informed her that all
the thousands of practice trials had now borne fruit. Her high
expectancies were reached, and the intrinsic joy she felt at that
moment was shared with the audience. In this case, the score of
10 also elicited an emotional reaction for perfection, and the gold
medal was hers. This information confirmed that which moments
earlier was communicated to her by her own bodily perceptions.

In all probability, the reasons for these two emotional reactions were different in nature. The first reaction, in this case positive, was a response to the gymnast's perception of how well the
planned routine met the expectancies that she set for herself in
terms of the performance *per se*. It should be pointed out that
these postperformance emotional reactions are not always spon-

taneous, since a false "competitive smile" is often feigned in order to persuade the judges that all went according to plan, when perhaps it did not. Gymnastics is a subjective sport, and this old trick sometimes works, but more often the judges can see through the thin affective veil.

The emotional reaction to the score may be of a different nature, since it would be to the consequences of the performance rather than to the performance itself. If the performance was good and the mark was better than expected, a positive reaction would be expected to this reward; the reverse reaction would also be expected for a low score. True emotional reactions to the score would be higher in intensity than those to the performance if the individual was more interested on how a score either could help the team placing or win a medal. Probably, the affective reactions to the score would be an uncontaminated natural reaction for the gymnasts, since they are no longer under the watchful gaze of the judges.

Again, differences might be expected between the emotional reactions of the men and the women if the experimental sport psychology research on this subject holds true (Alderman, 1974; Kane, 1972). Deci (1975) has also shown that women perceive intrinsic rewards (in this case, the satisfaction of performing well) and extrinsic rewards (the judges' score) in a different manner than do men. It would follow that their emotional reactions could also differ.

It would also be expected that the type and intensity of emotional reactions would be related to the ability level of the gymnasts, since the consequences of excellent performance in the highest ability levels are greater than those for the lower categories. Extreme personal satisfaction in its observable form of leaping, smiling, or laughing results when a never before performed movement is successfully executed. These performances are then rewarded in the form of medals, honor, or both, which again could result in emotional reactions that are more frequent than those observed when a well-deserved 8.5 score is flashed for a performer in lower ability level.

Finally, it is conceivable that different reactions could occur with athletes from different societies. Again, these differences could occur because one society is biologically more emotional than another. The classic population stereotype of this nature is the conception of Latins being hot tempered and Scandinavians, English, and Germans being cooler in temperament. There is also the possibility that the social contingencies within a society would cause its members to react differentially to the marks presented by the judges. Morton (1970) states, for example, that the Soviet athletes receive many benefits, including material ones, if they win in Olympic competition. In amateur sport in North America, success does not necessarily translate into material gain or even public recognition, so the consequences of success in the sport arena might elicit a lesser affective reaction from these athletes as compared to their Soviet counterparts.

In this chapter, these issues concerning the postperformance affective reactions of the gymnasts at the Montreal Olympics will be considered.

RECORDING PROCEDURES

The two classes of postperformance affective behaviors reported in this chapter were the reactions of gymnasts to their performance and the subsequent evaluation of this performance, i.e. the judges' score. Reactions to performance were operationally defined as those observable affective or emotional behaviors that took place during the five-second period between the gymnasts' landing from the dismount and their first steps taken to descend from the competition platform. Only behaviors that occurred prior to postperformance interaction with teammates or coach were considered in this portion of the study. The second class of behaviors, reactions to the evaluation, was operationally defined as those behaviors of emotionality that were observed during the five-second period that followed the presentation of the judges' scores. The scores were generally flashed about 30 to 45 seconds after termination of the performance.

Three types of post performance behaviors that were assessed in this study were positive and negative reactions, as well as a "no reaction" category. Coding of behaviors was based upon information derived from the states of total body and/or facial expressions. Positive reactions were operationally defined as being those behaviors that reflected satisfaction or pleasure with the previous performance or its evaluation: extended smiling, clapping the hands, waving enthusiastically, leaping, nodding the head, or running and skipping with joy.

Figure 6-1. Olga Korbut shows a positive emotional reaction to her balance beam performance.

Figure 6-2. Canada's Philip Delesalle shows no emotional reaction after his pommel horse routine.

Negative reactions were operationally defined as being those behaviors that reflected disappointment due to a poorly performed routine or a score that was believed to be too low: grimacing, frowning, shaking the head, dropping the shoulders, hanging the head, stamping or kicking the feet, or partial undressing with disgust. The category "no response" was operationally defined as being behaviors that demonstrated neither positive nor negative affective reactions but rather a dissociation from the previous performance or evaluation: returning without expression to the team bench, calmly arranging personal effects for the next event, or general apparent indifference to what has just previously occurred. One of the three response categories was coded and recorded by the trained observer for the assigned gymnast's reaction to performance (RP) and reaction to evaluation (RE).

The consensus between 82 parallel observations for both emotional reactions was calculated using Hall's (1974) procedures and were found to be 80.5% for the combined reactions, made up of 78.6% for the reaction to performance and 82.5% for the reaction to the evaluation.

Figure 6.3. East Germany's Angelika Hellmann reacts positively to her balance beam score.

Figure 6-4.   Lumilla Tourischeva shows no emotion after seeing her mark.

OVERALL PATTERNS OF EMOTIONAL REACTIONS

The relative frequencies of the observed emotional reactions to the gymnastic performance and to its evaluation are presented in table 6-I. When normalized for equal numbers of observations, the overall response pattern for the affective reactions to the performance is significantly different from that of the reaction to the scores $(\chi^2 \ (2) \ = 115.38, p < .01)$.

TABLE 6-I
FREQUENCY OF OBSERVED EMOTIONAL REACTIONS OF GYMNASTS
TO GYMNASTIC PERFORMANCE AND ITS EVALUATION

	Observed Reaction		
Cause of Reaction	Positive	Negative	No Reaction
Performance	212	47	433
Evaluation	62	47	438

The relative frequency of the positive and negative reactions decreased markedly from the reactions to performance to that for the evaluation. Positive response behaviors make up 30.6% of the

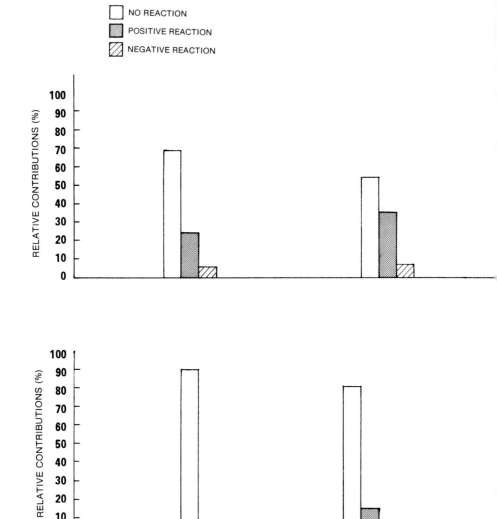

Figure 6-5. The patterns of the emotional reactions of the male and female gymnasts to the performance (A) and to the score (B) are shown. The reactions to the score were similar for both sexes, while the females showed greater positive reactions to the performance than the males.

former as compared to 12.1% for the latter. Negative emotional reactions to the performance make up 6.8% of all reactions while decreasing substantially to only 2.3% to the evaluation. The "no response" category is the predominant behavior in regard to the performance (62.5%) and to even a greater extent to its evaluation (85.4%).

SEX

The behavioral patterns for the affective reactions of the male and female gymnasts are shown in figure 6-5. The overall patterns for males and females when normalized for equal observations were found to be statistically different from one another (χ^2 (6) = 71.71, $p < .01$). The greatest sources of these overall differences were the positive reactions of the females both to the performance and its evaluation and the lack of response of the male gymnasts to the performance.

PERFORMANCE LEVEL

The observed affective reactions of the different performance levels are shown in figure 6-6. The emotional reactions to the performance between the different score brackets were shown to be significantly different for both the positive (χ^2 (4) = 27.79, $p < .01$) and negative reactions (χ^2 (4) = 10.20, $p < .05$), while the no response patterns were similar statistically. The greatest contributions to the overall differences for the positive reactions were the high incidence of occurrence for the best scoring group and the low incidence for the lowest performance group. The overall negative differences were primarily due to the great number of such reactions in the lowest performance bracket.

The affective reactions to the score were found to be similar across performance levels for the negative and no response categories, while overall differences were found in the positive reactions (χ^2 (4) = 31.01, $p < .01$). Again, these overall differences were primarily due to the low incidence of positive reactions of the poorest group and the high incidence of these behaviors for the best performance group.

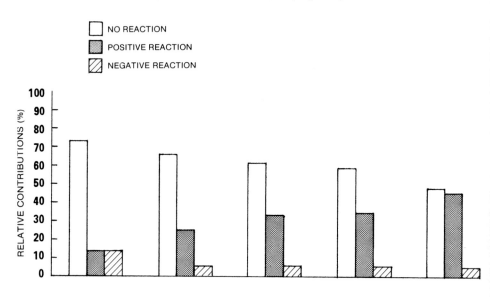

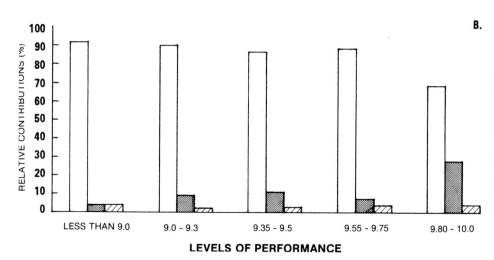

Figure 6-6. The positive emotional reaction to the performance generally increased with the attained score, while the negative responses were less pronounced.

SOCIETY

The emotional reactions of the gymnasts when regrouped in relation to their society of origin are shown in figure 6-7. When

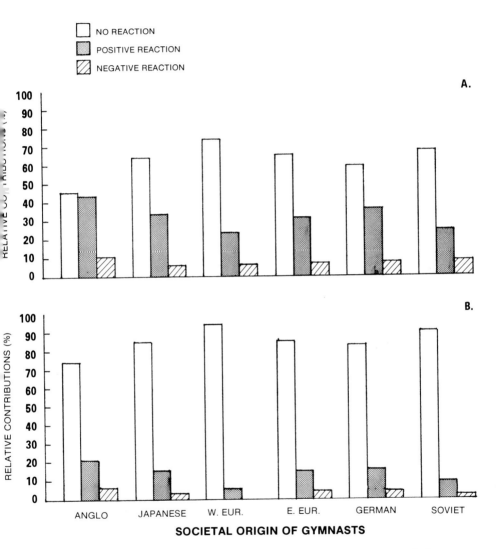

Figure 6-7. The great differences between the gymnasts of different societies in the patterns of positive response were due to the high incidence found with the Anglophones and western Europeans and the low level found with the Soviets.

each of the possible affective reactions is compared between societies, only the positive reactions to the performances were found
to be different statistically $(\chi^2 (5) = 11.03, p < .05)$. These overall differences were primarily because of the high incidence of
positive emotional reactions of the Anglophones and the western
Europeans and the low incidence of the same by the Soviet gymnasts.

DISCUSSION

In the chronological unfolding of the competitive gymnasts'
behavior patterns, the last observable actions in the drama are
the affective or emotional reactions to the just-completed routine
and to the score that the judges flash. The sequence is now complete. The gymnast moves on to the next station, begins to prepare himself or herself mentally and physically for the task demands of the following event, and the sequence of behavioral
patterns is repeated. Before looking at the implications of the
above data on affective reactions, a methodological point should
be underlined.

The usefulness of behavioral data, either as a means of con-
structing a portrait of a certain sport reality, as a test for theoretical constructs, or as a baseline for applied psychology techniques,
is limited by the ability of several trained observers to reliably
report the phenomena. In the present section, the overall percent
of agreement between the observers was 80.5% and was thus
judged acceptable in terms of Hall's (1974) criteria of reliability.
However, the consensus between observers for the reactions to performance was marginally inferior to Hall's 80% criterion, in-
dicating that emotional reactions of a gymnast to his/her performance might be more difficult to discern than the same behavioral
states as a reaction to the presented performance score. This
greater ambiguity in the observed emotional state for the performance reaction as compared to that of the evaluation is understandable, since the gymnast may choose, or be instructed, to
maintain a smiling "competitive face" until out of sight of the
judges. The intent of this behavior would be to induce the judges
to reciprocate this affect by increasing the performance score. Affective reactions to the score would not be contaminated by these

events and therefore might be easier to identify.

While certain similarities occurred in the emotional behavior patterns in regard to the performance and its evaluation, the analysis showed that the proportions of the different reactions were indeed different. This would tend to support the viewpoint that the gymnasts were reacting emotionally for different reasons. For one thing, the tendency to either react positively or negatively to the evaluation decreased as compared to the reactions to the performance. It could be offered that, in the first case, the gymnasts were making an emotional statement on the relative degree of satisfaction or dissatisfaction that they felt towards something over which they had control—the gymnastic routine. The reaction might tend to be stronger, since the gymnasts were ego-involved.

In regard to the score, they reacted to something that was no longer in their hands, and there might be a subsequently lower level of personal involvement and thus a lesser affective response. Thus, the locus of control of the stimulus that elicited the emotional response might have been the determining factor for its intensity. It could also be forwarded that the delay of 30 to 45 seconds between the performance and its evaluation could cause weakening of the emotional response over this duration. Given the importance of this competition, it was remarkable to note the number of gymnasts who never did consult the score at any time in the postperformance period. This, however, was not the case in the event finals, where the difference of hundredths of a point meant winning or losing a medal.

One mildly surprising observation was the predominance of the no response behavior and the low level of occurrence of positive and negative emotional reactions to the performance and especially to the evaluation. At least two explanations could be advanced for this lack of expressed emotion during this postperformance period. One could be that the gymnast is indifferent to his performance and its evaluation. However, the argument of indifference seems to be untenable given that the routines would seem to be ego-involving performances, based upon extensive daily training over a period of years. While there may be some habituation in the emotional reactions due to intensive competition and training, it would seem unlikely that this would override the intense situational emotion of an event taking place during the Olympic Games. Rejection of this indifference hypothesis would also seem supported by the fact that the frequency of the positive responses increases directly while the negative responses decrease as the scores get higher.

Similarly, these same phenomena were found as the gymnasts advanced from the preliminary to the final competitions. The more likely explanation for this high occurrence of nonemotional reactions is that the gymnasts are relatively accurate self-evaluators, using the movement feedback that they received during the routine in comparison with the scores that were assigned to similar performances in the past. Extreme emotional behaviors do not occur with great frequency at any level of performance, since even the highest scored gymnasts react emotionally in only 51.7% of performances immediately after dismounting and 30.8% of the time after receiving scores in the 9.75 to 10.0 range.

As was the case during the precompetitive period, the women during this postcompetitive phase demonstrated more behaviors of an emotional nature than did the men. In the sport psychology literature, opinion is divided on the subject of whether the female personality structure differs from that of the male athlete. Using personality tests, Kane (1972) reported that women athletes have been found to be more emotional than men. However, this increased emotionality should not be considered to be a weakness, but rather a mark of greater sensitivity to the environment. Alderman (1974) supports this position while adding that these differences probably are due to different socialization processes and are not biological in nature. Ogilvie (1967) and Vanek, Hosek, and Svoboda (1974) disagree, however, that there exist personality differences between the two sexes based upon extensive personality testing. The latter study was done on 824 elite Czechoslovakian athletes and differentiated between what they called emotional stability, or "excitability," and the anxiety of the athletes. While women were similar to men in emotionality, they were significantly more anxious. In the present case, it could be argued that the emotionality observed was elicited by the situation and did not reflect the more stable traits of the athletes' personalities as is measured by personality tests.

As has been repeatedly stated, there is very little systematic behavioral data on sport situations, with the few studies being related to feedback received during practice (Tharp & Gallimore, 1976; Brunelle et al., 1978) and competition (Salmela, 1979). In the present study, for each of the pre– and postcompetitive phases, differences between the sexes were found. Interpretation of these differences at this moment is speculative, but nevertheless, this speculation does point to new directions for investigation.

One promising alternative for the explanation of these differential patterns between the male and female emotional reaction is suggested by Kane (1972) when he attributes these sex differences in a positive manner. Rather than considering higher emotion to be a sign of ego weakness, it is positively considered to be an indication that women are more sensitive to their surroundings than are men. After all, is it not more natural to be emotionally uplifted after having competed well during an Olympic Games or to be visibly saddened by not having performed to one's fullest at this moment of truth?

In a recent book, Goffman (1979) points out that women are socialized into inferior and subservient positions to men, as exemplified by typical advertisements in newspapers and magazines. Based upon physiognomic and postural analyses of men and women in ads, he refers to women as being portrayed as "flooding out" of situations by retreating into emotions such as fear, horror, shyness, or mirth. Broyard (1979) in a review of Goffman's book interpreted these spontaneous and antic positions of the women similarly to Kane (1972), as indicative of being closely in touch with the environment, as compared to men who ". . . appear to be monolithically rigid, naively serious, absurdly mobilized against imaginary threats, afraid to lie down, to lose themselves in pleasure, to try on roles, to mu   or speculate." (p. 12).

A similar interpretation can be made of the male gymnasts' relative lack of emotional response in such an emotionally charged atmosphere, as the result of being socialized into not showing appropriate emotion. In a recent television presentation of the World Cup of gymnastics from Tokyo, the initial lead-in to the program referred to an American "first" in gymnastics, that of a

U.S. male gymnast being in first place going into an event final. The cameras followed young Bart Conner through his apparently faultless routine to the dismount. Upon landing, no emotional reaction was observed. When the score was flashed that indicated that he had won, no signs of emotion could then be seen. The announcer remarked that he probably was very happy but did not show it, for whatever reason. In a subsequent interview, Conner was very excited and showed to the delight of the audience the boyish emotion that goes along with winning a world championship, but that might not be proper behavior on the gym floor. Exceptions to wearing this mask of nonemotionality are the male gymnasts Gienger of West Germany, Szajna of Poland, and Tzukahara of Japan, all of whom are visibly happy upon having done well. As a result, they communicate this joy to the crowd, and possibly to the judges, and thus become favorites of both groups.

One other notable exception to the stoic postperformance reactions of the male gymnasts has recently been observed with the gymnasts from Cuba. At both the 1978 World Championships in Strasbourg and the 1979 Pan American Games in Puerto Rico, most performances were followed by joyous leaping, hugging, and broad smiling. It was refreshing to observe, and one must wonder whether this will be the new trend in postcompetitive behaviors.

These differences in emotional reactions between the sexes might also have been due to the age of the female gymnasts, who were on the average five years younger than the males. It is of interest that the superstar of the 1976 Olympic Games, Nadia Comaneci, was enigmatic, and thus of interest to the world, because of the fact that this young child showed no visible emotion, a behavior that is not typically associated with young children who succeed in sport. This athletic wonder played childishly with a doll at the Olympic Village but worked as a serious grownup while she practiced and competed. In fact, she had to be coached and persuaded by a team sport psychologist to show an emotional reaction to the thunderous applause of the crowd after her perfect performances (see Chapter 6 title photo).

The level of performance also was shown to have an effect on the emotional reactions. As might be expected, the frequency of positive responses increased with the increase in scores, while there was a concomitant decrease in the frequency and proportion of negative responses. Emotional reactions to the score, however, did not increase in such a simplistic fashion. For those who scored less than 9.0, there was an understandably low level of positive responses and a higher level of negative reactions. For those gymnasts whose scores fell within the middle range, there was a decrease in positive reactions with increasing scores, along with an increase in negative reactions. It seems that the closer the gymnasts were to the top scores, the greater was their frustration and disappointment in not attaining the goal. This understandable increase in emotionality as the goal was being approached was also evidenced when the behaviors were grouped according to the importance of the competition. The number of both positive and negative responses increased as the gymnasts progressively advanced from the preliminaries to the all-around finals and to the event finals. It was somewhat surprising that the emotional reactions were so closely tied to the performance level. In most cases, prior to the competition, the gymnasts have a fairly accurate expectancy of where they will finish, based upon earlier competitions. Since the number of missed routines was fairly low, one might think that most gymnasts would be content to do as well as they could at this important competition. In a way, it was unfortunate that the intermediate level gymnasts did not show as much contentment with the realization of a personal best performance as did the medal winners in the top category.

The regrouping of the emotional responses in terms of the society of origin of the gymnasts provides striking information on how the external competition variable, besides the movement feedback from the performance itself, can influence the postperformance emotional responses. The Anglophone classification was made up primarily of observations on the American and Canadian gymnasts, the group that was observed to exhibit the greatest frequency and proportion of emotional responses to the performance and, by far, the greatest frequency of negative reactions to the scores. This might be explained by the fact that these gymnasts' ability levels were not comparable to the eventual winners, yet they were recipients of tremendous crowd and media support. Expectations for success might have been unduly raised because of the milieu of the competition, which resulted in positive emotional responses to the performance and disappointed reactions to the scores.

The high level of positive emotional responses by the western Europeans is more difficult to explain by means of the situational variables. Support by the crowd was not particularly strong for these gymnasts, since they were neither hometown heroes nor were they among the best performers with but one exception, Boerio of France. It could be that their biological makeup was of a more emotional variety, and perhaps the Latin nature of these Spanish, Italian, and French gymnasts was the reason for this display of emotional behavior.

The Soviets, as was the case with the other behavioral variables, showed emotional patterns that were different from all of the other societies. While they are extremely competent gymnasts, winning the women's team title and placing second to the Japanese for the men, their positive response pattern to performance was significantly lower than that of the other nations. In their case, success did not necessarily result in positive emotional responses. Hanin (1977) mentioned that this nonemotionality was a learned behavior that allowed the gymnasts to withdraw into a competitive shell in which their attention was focused on the performance details and not upon extraneous events such as the score. Given these practices, it is understandable why Soviet gymnasts such as Olga Korbut and Nelli Kim were perceived as being different from their teammates and were such crowd favorites.

Aside from the effects of sex, performance level, and societal differences that contributed to the complex equation required to explain differential reactions to gymnastic performance and its evaluation, recent work in causal attribution for success and failure in sport (Roberts, 1975) indicates that the nature of the task difficulty would cause variations in the emotional response in the postperformance period. Pommel horse and horizontal bar, the apparatus that are judged to be the most difficult in men's gymnastics, are those that caused the greatest frequency of emotional reactions to performance. Pommel horse has been shown to tax the gymnast's information-processing capacities to the fullest

(Salmela, 1979e) and could be said to require the greatest effort to remain upon the apparatus, while the vault is a hit-or-miss event, where luck might play a greater role. A greater emotional reaction could be hypothesized for the former task demands than for the latter. This relation is more clear on the women's events where the difficult balance beam event caused the greatest frequency of emotional responses to both the performance and to the score, while the vault event has the lowest frequency of the same.

Taken as a whole, the postperformance affective reactions that were observed during the gymnastic competition at the Olympics raise many more questions than they answer. Several avenues of research appear open that could make important contributions to the understanding of these emotional reactions to high level performance and its evaluation. The evaluation of these same emotional states using sport-specific tests similar to those used by Martens (1977) for state anxiety, as well as interview techniques (Smoll, Smith, & Hunt, 1977), could be undertaken in order to better understand the effects of sex, performance level, and society of origin on these behaviors. Systematic observation of the many elite sporting events can provide a wealth of information that can serve to complement existing data on performance. These initial steps of behavioral assessment can provide tools for identifying problem behaviors, controlling these behaviors by modification techniques, and allowing experimental constructs in sport psychology to be generated and evaluated.

POINTS OF INTEREST

• The reason that gymnasts reacted with a greater frequency of emotional behaviors to their performances rather than their score may be that they have an accurate capacity for self-evaluation. Upon dismounting, they are happy to have completed their routine successfully. They also have a fairly good idea of their potential score based upon past experience and upon the information that their kinesthetic system has brought them during the routine, so that the score is but confirming what they already know and their emotional response is less intense.

• A movement artist, such as a ballet dancer, invariably smiles to her public upon completing a performance in order to give closure to the communication process with the audience. Possibly the reason that there is such a high level of postperformance nonemotional reactivity by gymnasts is that they do not want the judges to know that they are happy to have successfully completed their routine, which may have been due to some kind of luck and may result in lower scores.

• Emotional reactions seemed to be more intense for those events that are usually considered to be the most difficult. There were a greater number of positive reactions from gymnasts having just completed routines on the pommel horse and balance beam. These smiles were probably smiles of relief. It would not, however, hurt the sport of gymnastics, nor any other type of elite athletics, to show the general public that happiness can be compatible with high intensity competition and the attainment of excellence. Many critics only show the darker side of what can be a pleasureable experience.

PART THREE

Chapter 7

MALE AND FEMALE COMPETITIVE BEHAVIOR PATTERNS

What behavioral differences between Warren Long and Sherry Hawco of Canada are of significance?

Summary

In this chapter, the pre- and postcompetitive behaviors of the male and female gymnasts are considered. Behavior patterns for the men and women gymnasts differ, and do so consistently, during both phases of the osbervation. The women gymnasts spent significantly more of their preparation time in contact with their coaches and received a greater incidence of positive feedback from this source. The men demonstrated greater contact with teammates during these two phases of the competition. The women showed greater incidence of emotional behaviors, which probably reflected anxiety, during the preparation period than did the men; the women also showed a greater incidence of positive and negative emotional reactions to their own performances. Both groups showed equally low levels of emotional reactions to the score.

THE OLYMPIC competitions in gymnastics tend to be the key historical moments upon which hinge the future tendencies in the sport for the next period of four years. Over the last three Olympiads, varied changes in the technical style as well as in the accompanying behaviors of the gymnasts have occurred, but most markedly on the women's side. In Mexico in 1968, the noble beauty of Czechoslovakia's Vera Caslavska captured the eye of the world's media as she defeated her Soviet counterparts with stately elegance. The militarily caused tensions between the two countries were resolved this time in favor of Czechoslovakia.

This image of the full, mature, serious woman gymnast was carried on to the 1972 Munich Games, as the stately Soviet gymnast Ludmilla Tourischeva won the all-around competition. But a foreshadowing of future events occurred with the presence of 17-year-old Olga Korbut. Not only did she astound the world with her extreme levels of difficulty, which some thought bordered on circus stunts, but she set off a revolution in the sport that attracted younger and younger gymnasts. Her diminutive size allowed smaller, younger females to have an international sport celebrity after whom they could model their own behaviors. While gymnastics was already a sport in which it was socially acceptable for girls to compete (Metheny, 1965), now it appeared probable that success and recognition could also occur within a reasonable length of time for aspiring candidates. Thousands of young girls began to participate in the sport, attracted by Olga's childlike image that was highlighted by pigtails, a very real smile, and very real tears. The youthful image and the emotional contact that Olga represented started a trend towards the "child-champion" that was to be epitomized at Montreal.

At the Montreal Games, the story was all Nadia Comaneci, the 15-year-old *wunderkind,* who not only represented lithe female youth but also athletic perfection. Nadia was the first gymnast ever to receive a score of 10 in Olympic competition, and this on repeated occasions. The confrontation of the former media darling, Olga, with the new Rumanian sensation, Nadia, was a fizzle. Olga was outclassed. Nadia added to the evolution of the female gymnastic image by combining the playful, but perfectly executed, childlike poses of Olga when competing, with a serious demeanor before and after her routine that reminded observers of someone much older than her years. This newest step of being seriously competitive at a very young age again started a trend to prepubescent female gymnasts working at their sport in a serious, almost businesslike fashion.

Now the question can be posed of how do women fit within the competitive sport structure, and is it any different from the same situation for men? Within the context of the present study, the authors are limited to analyzing the patterns of behaviors that were observed before and after competing and relating these behaviors to research on sex roles in sport.

SOCIAL BEHAVIORS

Zoble (1972) has reviewed much of the research done on femininity and achievement in sport. She points out that the role of the female in sport, as in other aspects of life, is rapidly evolving to one where excellence itself and the fierce determination necessary for its attainment is more socially acceptable. Perhaps the movement towards younger and younger female gymnasts has facilitated the adoption of this new gender identity for achievement by women, since the self-concept of the woman and her expected roles are still in the formative stage. Since the average age of the women gymnasts was over five years younger than that of the men (18.0 versus 23.4 years), it is not clear whether the observed differences between the sexes were, in fact, due to gender or to age. Probably both played a role.

The social behaviors during the preparation period and during the feedback stage after the performance were quite distinct, and consistently so, for the men and the women. During the preparation phase the men were in the physical presence of their teammates more often than were the women and, following the performance, the men received substantially more congratulatory feedback from their peers as compared to the women. The women were, in turn, more often in the presence of their coach before competing and received more feedback from her upon dismounting.

If one adopts the point of view that different socialization processes occur for women gymnasts than men, these relational differences with one's teammates have some support in the psychological literature. Bardwick (1971), in her book on the psychology of women, notes that females were more aggressive to one another than were males in the same situation. However, the forms that this aggression took were more subtle and included gossip, verbal slams, and withdrawal of friendship. This last point could be the source of the present findings that the women gymnasts were not with their teammates as frequently during preparation and tended to congratulate their peers less after the completion of the routine. Overall, the women performed without receiving any form of feedback at all more often than did the men. Perhaps this was another instance of withdrawal of friendship.

The social role of the coach appeared to be different for the men as compared to the women. The male coach was in the physical presence of the men during both the preparation and the feedback phase of the competition less than was the female coach with the women. Bardwick again points out that dependency on adults is more acceptable in young girls than it is for males and may result in a greater need in the females for seeking approval from adults. Again, the female gymnasts were the recipients of more positive feedback from their coach than were the males. This greater dissociation between the male coach and gymnasts may have also been partially due to certain *machismo* tendencies in the male coaches, by which the overt showing of sensitivity to another male is perceived as a sign of weakness.

If, however, one adopts the viewpoint that it is the age difference rather than the difference of gender that resulted in the disparity between the social behavioral profiles of the men and women gymnasts, other sources of support must be sought. It may well be that the older male gymnasts possessed to a greater degree the capacity to live the competition experience within a positive perspective where cohesion or personal contact was valued more than team rivalry. The younger female gymnasts might have been more stimulus-bound by the tasks of the competition and were not yet automated enough to prepare for competition while embracing the social needs of their teammates as well. It is unfortunate, however, that at this important period in their young lives they do go without being reinforced positively to the same extent as the men. The minimal effort required would seem to be well expended. Since a gymnast's career in elite sport often ends after the Olympic Games, this moment would be better crystalized in memory with a small pat on the back, than by being ignored.

EMOTIONAL BEHAVIORS

The female gymnasts observed in this study exhibited a greater incidence of what were termed emotional behaviors than the men, during both the pre– and postcompetitive phases. All other behaviors, except the ideomotor ones, were observed to be the same. It is at this point that some of the inherent limitations of behavior observation should be underlined. Baer, Risley, and Wolf (1968) suppose that observable behaviors and the ways of controlling them are the essential elements in applied psychology rather than attempting to get at the internalized intentions or motives that cause them. However, in the case of what are here termed emotional behaviors, it is possible that high emotion is occurring without being apparent through observable behaviors, or conversely that "emotional" behaviors are exhibited without being based upon underlying emotion. Additional measures must complement observation, such as interviews or measuring of physiological responses, if these questions are to be replied to with confidence.

One further distinction should be made regarding these emotional behaviors before specific comparisons are made between the male and the female gymnasts observed at Montreal. This distinction is one that Spielberger (1966) made in terms of two dimensions of anxiety, state and trait. State anxiety is "characterized by subjective, consciously perceived feelings of apprehension and tension, accompanied by or associated with activation or arousal of the autonomic nervous system" (p. 17). This could be the situational anxiety provoked by being at the Olympic Games, by being on an apparatus that is perceived to be more difficult than another, or by being in the finals rather than in a preliminary competition. Trait anxiety, however, "is a motive or acquired behavioral disposition that predisposes an individual to perceive a wide range of objectively non-dangerous circumstances as threatening, and to respond to these with state anxiety reactions disproportionate in intensity to the magnitude of the objective danger" (p. 17). This refers to the emotional makeup specific to an individual's sex or culture that has either been learned or is genetically determined.

In this perspective, opinion is divided as to whether the emotional makeup of men and women is different and as to the causes of these differences, if any. Alderman (1974) believes that women have basically different personality profiles than men, although it is forwarded that these variances are not biological in nature but are due to the fact that socialization processes into sport are not the same. Kane (1972) reported that women tended to be more emotional than men, based upon personality tests. He did, however, add that this increased level of emotionality was not the result of a weak ego but was due to an increased level of sensitivity to the environment. Vanek, Hosek, and Svoboda (1974), based upon a large sample of female Czechoslovakian athletes, differentiated between emotionality, where men and women were similar, and anxiety, which the women exhibited more of than the men. Ogilvie (1967) reflected a somewhat different opinion when he stated that the personality traits of women were "highly consistent with those of males" (p. 48).

Most recently, Restak (1979) has reviewed extensive literature on the brain behavior of boys and girls that shows that definite biological differences do occur between the sexes in terms of both cognitive and motor activity. Present educational practices are shown to discriminate against both sexes in different ways, since they are not always sensitive to the varied biological make-up of boys and girls. Restak shows that girls have advantages in the early years of school because the curriculum favors their greater linguistic skills, while the boys' inherent mastery of spatial and conceptual tasks gives them distinct advantages in certain college entrance exams that are weighted on these dimensions. The danger of ignoring these brain-sex differences by confusing biology with sociology in a manner similar to Alderman's (1974) argument above is underlined by Restak as one where wishful thinking is substituted for scientific fact.

In the present case, all evidence points to marked behavioral differences between the male and female gymnasts, with the females exhibiting more "emotionality" than the males. As was mentioned in regard to the social states, the factor of age could have played a deciding role in these behavioral differences. If, as Kalvora (1975) points out, experience or skill levels will tend to reduce anxiety, then the five-year average difference in ages of the men and women participants may explain the increased incidence of emotional behaviors by the women during the preparation phase of the competition. It is plausible that the males' increased competitive experience would cause lower levels of anxiety. It is also possible that it is less acceptable for their *machismo* image to anxiously pace back and forth in order to relieve their emotional tensions as did the females. Again, it could be a combination of lower levels of learned or inhibited emotional dispositions of the males and the greater social constraints not to show emotion that contributed to these differences in behaviors.

The incidence of emotional reaction to the performance was again higher for the female gymnasts than for the males. While termed emotional, these responses probably did not share a common psychological base with the emotional behaviors exhibited during preparation. The former behaviors were emotional reactions to performance success or failure, contaminated slightly by smiling competitive faces in order to sway judges, while the latter were manifestations of possible anxiety, nervousness, or fear preceding the performance and reflected neither the emotions of joy nor sadness observed after the performance.

It was striking that for the men there was such a high occurrence of no emotional reactions to the performance. It is puzzling that the male gymnast wears a mask of indifference in a situation that may be one of the highest emotional peaks of his life. The comments of Broyard (1979) regarding rigid, non-antic behaviors and postures of males in emotional situations depicted in advertisements may be appropriate here. Rather than expressing a calm *machismo* sense of cool, these behaviors may represent an inability to cope with the emotional reality of a very exciting situation. It is but human to express joy and sadness in reaction to a performance that may have taken up to 15,000 hours of work to realize.

In this same vein, the higher emotional reactions of the women are interpreted within the spirit of what Kane (1972) offers, as being an indication of greater sensitivity to the environment rather than having a weak ego. The potential for artistic emotional expression would seem to naturally go beyond the temporal point of the dismount, so that the communication with the audience could be complete. What is surprising is that not more of it goes on, as in other expressive modes such as the theater or dance, since it is so well received.

Olga Korbut's popularity was in a large part due to her ability to show and share her immediate emotional states, whether positive or negative, with the crowd. Nadia Comaneci was an enigma since, even after she demonstrated gymnastic perfection, it could be seen that her smile was turned on mechanically, the work of the team psychologist. Nevertheless, the crowd loved to have some emotional contact with these young artistic gymnasts, whether spontaneous or preprogrammed.

Finally, in the case of both the male and female gymnasts, very low frequencies of either positive or negative emotional reactions were observed to the performance evaluations. Besides being good evaluators of the information coming from their own bodies, it appeared that the gymnasts drew great pleasure from the intrinsic reward of their own performance and were less preoccupied by the psychological pat on the back that the judges' scores represented, at least in those situations where a medal was not at stake.

While the pre– and postcompetitive behavior patterns observed do find some support from the sport psychology literature on women in sport (Harris, 1972), there still remains a series of questions that have to be considered. What are the relative roles of biological versus cultural factors in the behavior patterns of the sexes? How do these patterns change with growth? And most importantly for the present study, how do the individual coaches and gymnasts perceive their own behaviors on the floor, and what meanings do they attribute to them?

POINTS OF INTEREST

- The fact that the women consistently demonstrated higher levels of emotional behaviors than the men, both before and after their routines, could be explained by several different reasons or by a combination of them all. It may be that women are biologically more emotional than men. Or it may be that women have not yet learned to be "at home" in the competitive setting, which has been traditionally the domain of the male. Again, it could be the result of the fact that the women were, on the average, five years younger than the men and possibly not yet emotionally "mature."
- An alternate explanation of the differences in emotional behaviors between the sexes is that the women react more naturally in face of the high excitement of the Olympic Games. The men may be more socially constrained not to show emotion. This emotional indifference on their part is but a veil and is not necessarily a demonstration of positive affective control.
- It is not yet known what effect the decreasing ages of the gymnasts, especially in the case of the women, will have on the ability to maintain emotional control in these high stress situations. It may be that the gymnasts may have advantages in being young, since they may not perceive all of the stress such as political gain and peer or media pressure causing agents at that age that may emotionally affect older competitors.
- Both before and after the performance, the relationship between the competing gymnast and the coach and teammates seems to be different for men and women. The further study of coach-athlete relationships is warranted, especially when the coach and the athlete are of different sexes. It may be that male coaches should adopt different coaching styles for men and for women,

although the appropriate dimensions for these differences are not immediately apparent.

• It is clear that males and females interact differently with their teammates, the males tending to spend more time with them as compared to their female counterparts. A tentative statement of these relations of a social nature based upon the observed behaviors might be that the males showed greater cohesion while the females demonstrated greater rivalry.

Chapter 8

CROSS-CULTURAL COMPETITIVE
BEHAVIOR PATTERNS

What behavioral differences exist between female
gymnasts Schlegel of Canada and Okazaki of Japan?

131

Summary

In this chapter, the pre- and postcompetitive behaviors of gymnasts originating from six societies are compared. The behavior patterns between the gymnasts of these societies showed large differences, which had a degree of consistency across both the pre- and the postcompetitive phases. The German and the Japanese coaches demonstrated the most social contact with their gymnasts and also provided the highest levels of feedback. The Anglophone and the western European gymnasts had similarily high levels of social contact with teammates. The Soviets were predominantly alone prior to competing and received little feedback from their associates upon dismounting. The incidence of emotional behaviors of Anglophones and western Europeans was low prior to competing but was very high afterwards, while the reverse was true for the Soviets.

GYMNASTIC TECHNIQUE is often named after the individual gymnast who first performed the movement in international competition. As a result, we have the Comaneci dismount on the uneven parallel bars, the Tzukahara vault, the Stalder shoot on the horizontal bar, and the Thomas flair on the pommel horse. Similarly, certain countries have initiated specific techniques that have left the gymnastic nomenclature a legacy of Czech circles and Russian loops on the pommel horse, German giants and Finn stemme swings on the horizontal bar, and Russian or Japanese somersaults on the floor exercises. Now it may also be possible to attach national or societal labels on the types of preparatory, social, and emotional behaviors that surround the actual athletic performance of the gymnasts. It could be that there is a Soviet preparation technique, an American set of social behaviors, and a Japanese system for feedback in gymnastics.

Caution, however, must be taken in the interpretation of behaviors from another culture, since these perceptions are colored by ethnocentric tendencies to see things as they are in the observer's own culture. Walter Lippman states in Eysenck's (1953) classic book, *The Uses and Abuses of Psychology,* that in the observation of a new environment, one tends to focus on the elements that one's culture has already defined in terms of the stereotypes inherent in the culture. Brown (1965) observed that besides the ethnocentricity that is objectionable in the formation of cultural stereotypes, there is also the implication that these traits are inborn and invariant for these large groups. Both of these characteristics have permitted stereotypes to become dangerous tools for racial discrimination and even war. It can be shown that ethnic stereotypes are, in fact, dependent on geographical position or political alliance and will vary from era to era, depending on the particular political or economic circumstances.

In the present study, the cultural behavioral patterns were presented to the reader for inspection, and interpretative value judgments were guardedly kept to a minimum. However, the Canadian cultural perspective of the authors from which these comments are made, whatever that entity may be, should be kept in consideration.

While caution must be maintained in attaching values to behaviors that do not resemble those of the observers, there is little doubt that cross-cultural differences would be observed in the competition behaviors of athletes because of these same variations in social contingencies and reinforcement patterns in each society. As Roberts and Sutton-Smith (1966) point out, play, and in this case sport, are cultural inventions rather than biological universals. Different cultures would presumably mold the functional and social behaviors that occur in elite competition to reflect the prevailing traits, values, expectations, and degree of social control particular to the respective societies. Zurcher and Meadow (1967) related these values to the ritualistic behaviors that accompanied the dominant sports of two cultures, supposedly as a function of the national characteristics of these nations. If it can be assumed that different cultures do impose particularly sport-related traits and values on their athletes, whether voluntarily or involuntarily, these influences would presumably be translated into observable behaviors.

Overall consideration of the four pre– and postcompetition categories revealed certain communalities in the consistent patterns of the observed behaviors across the cultures. The precompetitive social states and the postcompetitive feedback patterns are both related to the degree of social interaction between the athletes and the coaches at these important moments. While gymnastics is a parallel performance type of competition that does not depend directly upon team unity, other important human dimensions, such as increasing the levels of self-worth by sharing of feelings at these peak moments, may result from closer team cohesion. On the other hand, the preparatory states and emotional reactions to the performance and its evaluation are behaviors that may be more specific to personal idiosyncracy but may still be culturally influenced. With this in mind, the individual and social behaviors have been treated separately.

SOCIAL BEHAVIORS

Overall, the social states of the gymnasts during the preparatory phase showed great cultural differences. The exception was the state of being alone, the predominant state that was necessary in order to accomplish the large number of instrumental acts required for gymnastic competition. The social state of being physically together with one's teammates varied enormously, with the western Europeans being for a large part with others while the Soviets spent less than 1% of this preparation period with either their coaches or their teammates. Explanation of this social relationship of the western Europeans may be due partially to greater team cohesion as a result of greater familiarization with athletes within the boundaries of smaller countries. Lack of cohesion or even rivalry on the team, if this is the case with the Soviets, is not necessarily a bad thing, as Luchen (1970) points out, especially with these individual sports in which team cooperation is not necessary for success. In fact, Hanin (1977) pointed out that this was a mark of the Soviet gymnasts' independence.

Particular patterns emerged in terms of interaction of gymnasts and with their associates. The Anglophones carried on the most social intercourse with their teammates, which might have had something to do with the fact that they were at home, relatively at ease, and not really fighting for the medals to any extent. Again the Soviets demonstrated more detached behaviors during this phase, interacting very little with teammates or coaches. From the data on the interaction with the coaches, it seems that some individuals played quite an active counselling role in this precompetitive period, although the coaches mainly left the gymnasts alone. For example, the Japanese (12.8%) and German (9.7%) coaches were in close contact with their gymnasts as compared to similar measures on the Soviet coaches (.7%). It was obvious that certain cultures emphasized the importance of team "togetherness." These gymnasts seemed to stay in close proximity to one another during most phases of the competition, while others did not emphasize these same team structures. The role of the coach varied between that of scorekeeper, counsellor, equipment adjuster, or figurehead from culture to culture.

The feedback behaviors, especially in terms of their source, were interestingly correlated with the patterns of behaviors of the social states. For example, the western European gymnasts, who received the most feedback from teammates, also spent the most time in their presence prior to competing. Similarly, the German gymnasts, who spent a fair amount of time actively exchanging with the coach before their routines, were positively reinforced to a great extent by the coach at the end of their routines. Taken overall, it appeared that the Western societies, whether it be the Anglophone, western European, or the "westernized easterners" from Japan, gave the greatest amounts of positive feedback, not often letting a compatriot finish without immediate social reinforcement. The eastern European and Soviet gymnasts, however, were at the other end of the scale in terms of the observed patterns, in that they provided this feedback the least. It should, however, be added that these athletes could be seen to be attentive while their companions were competing and often applauded on the completion of the routine, but they very seldom communicated directly with gymnasts by the behavioral definitions in this study.

What, then, can be said about the social behaviors of the gymnasts from the various societies, if it is accepted that the societal values and mores determine their behaviors in play and sport?

It would be unjust to say that the western Europeans are friendly and warm towards each other while the Soviets are distant and uncaring to their associates, based upon their physical distance or their congratulatory pats on the back. However, it also could not be said that being distant from one's teammates is a prerequisite for success in order to maximize performance, as Hanin (1977) suggested, since the equally successful Japanese and Germans demonstrated closer relations during their brief period. Other measures related to cohesion and performance must complement behavior observation procedures in order to sort this out. But if being close and being distant get the same job accomplished, is not close better?

EMOTIONAL BEHAVIORS

No behavioral differences were found between the societies for the relative contributions of any of the preparatory behaviors except for those that were termed emotional.

As might be expected during the period that immediately precedes competition in gymnastics, a large percentage of the time was spent on the instrumental behaviors of chalking, adjusting, walking, and manipulating within the limited confines of the site. It also follows that the patterns of preparation, whether they be of a mental, ideomotor, or motor nature, would tend to be culturally universal, since the tasks were similar for all gymnasts concerned.

The Soviets performed the greatest number of acts that were operationally defined as being emotional behaviors, such as pacing back and forth, loosening up, or demonstrating nervous tics. Given the overall strength of their performances, these behaviors may have been related to high personal expectancies and resulting anxiety. However, Japanese and German gymnasts, who also did well, did not demonstrate this same frequency of emotional behaviors. These tendencies, then, might be due to the reinforcement patterns of receiving additional benefits within the Soviet society, which results in anxious behaviors in their attempts to do well at these international competitions (Morton, 1970). Whatever the reason for these behavior patterns, it cannot be ignored that the frequency of occurrence of emotional behaviors by the Soviets was 10 times that of the western European gymnasts.

Of the four behavior classifications studied, the postcompetitive emotional reactions showed the greatest cross-cultural communalities. Only the levels of positive emotional reactions to the performance were shown to vary significantly between the cultures. The Anglophones and eastern Europeans showed the greatest levels of positive emotional responses, as compared to the lowest levels displayed by the Soviet and Japanese gymnasts. It is possible that the local support for the North American gymnasts by the large numbers of Canadian and American spectators may have falsely boosted their reactions to their performance. While this ebullience was somewhat translated into positive reactions to the score, there was also some indication that the Anglophones' relatively low level of performance proficiency did not warrant all of this support, as evidenced by the highest incidence of negative responses to the evaluations. The high incidence of positive performance reactions by the eastern Europeans may have been less situational in nature and due to intelligent training on their part. Smiling at the end of a performance may have been predetermined and done to induce the judges to reciprocate this affect by increasing the scores. The low incidence of positive emotional reactions by the Soviet gymnasts, when compared to the high incidence of what could be termed anxious emotional behaviors, indicated that a common psychological phenomenon was not at the base of their competition predisposition. Perhaps the Japanese dictum "cry in practice, laugh in competition" is reversed for the Soviets.

The cross-cultural differences in behaviors of a social and emotional nature seem to consistently demonstrate themselves during the various phases of the elite competition process, thus lending some support to the stability of these psychological phenomena. Further means of considering the intentions behind these behaviors when coupled with additional observation on these and other sport phenomena may contribute to the unravelling of sport behaviors and their cultural determinants as outlined by Morton (1970) when he stated, "Analysis of a nation at play reveals the stuff of its social fabric and value system, and tells us much about other facets of political and economic life, especially in modern society" (p. 13).

POINTS OF INTEREST

• The prevailing values inherent within the different societies from which the gymnasts originate have probably contributed to the grossly different cross-cultural behavior patterns that emerge.

• The Japanese and German coaches seemed to play the greatest active coaching roles of all of the mentors from the participating societies. This may reflect certain paternalistic tendencies within these cultures. When the comparison is made with the Soviet coaches, who spent less than 1% of their time with the athletes, one must ask oneself, "What is the essential coaching role that should be adopted for optimal performance in elite competition?" Or does active coaching need to go at all?

• The types of social feedback seemed to be split down the political left-right continuum. The gymnasts from the socialist eastern European countries or from the Soviet Union received lower levels of feedback, while the capitalistic Anglophone, western European, and Japanese gymnasts received more total instances of postperformance support. It may well be that the rewards in the western societies were but those that were received on the floor of the competition, while more lasting benefits occurred in the eastern socialist societies once the gymnasts returned home.

• By far the most striking phenomena of all of the cross-cultural observations was the singularly different behavior patterns of the Soviet gymnasts. These differences occurred in terms of the social contact and emotional behaviors before competing as well as the way that they reacted emotionally and dispensed feedback after the performance. The reasons for these discrepancies in behavior are not obvious, since they were not consistently similar to the behaviors of the gymnasts from societies that were on a comparable performance level or that shared a common socio-political position.

Chapter 9

A RETROSPECTIVE LOOK AT
GYMNASTIC BEHAVIORS

What has been observed, and where does it lead?
Nelli Kim again begins the competitive behavioral
process in 1978 at the World Championships in
Strasbourg, France.

AT EACH Olympiad, one never ceases to wonder at the tremendous advances that have been made in sport performance, and nowhere is it more evident than in artistic gymnastics. As the technicians leave the competition arena, the question always arises, Where can we go from here? At that moment, one is certain that the ultimate in gymnastic perfection has been reached. The addition of more difficulty or risk will surely tip the delicate balance from movement artistry to the reckless performance of hair-raising carnival stunts if it is not tempered with virtuosity. Yet, at the succeeding Olympiad, there appears Nadia Comaneci, whose routines are even more risky and difficult than were those impossible tricks that Olga Korbut performed in Munich, while being performed with more grace and sureness. And even now, Nadia has been surpassed.

Are we not soon approaching the margins that limit human capacity to perform? The elite gymnasts are becoming younger and younger, so young that the women's best performances are occurring during the prepubescent years (Salmela, 1979d). Will there be a cutoff point where advantages gained by lithe, light body structures will be traded off against the inability of the young mind to absorb the psychological stress? Or is the psyche at that age more resilient to such forces than was ever believed? When will the high information-processing demands of certain events exceed the gymnast's capacity to deal faultlessly with all of the signals coming from body to brain (Salmela, 1979e)? Or when will fear of injury prevent the twisting quadruple somersault from being performed? Speculations on the impossibility of performance of a particular move on any event would surely prove as inadequate as were those of the great British gymnast Nick Stuart (1964), whose "dream routines" are now being performed almost without exception.

In the same manner, it is possible to focus on those behaviors that precede and follow the routines themselves. Will these patterns evolve in the same way that the gymnastics routines advance? Are there any behavioral goals towards which the patterns observed at the twenty-first Olympiad in Montreal could progress? What would be the criteria against which the gymnasts' behaviors

could be compared, so that he or she would ultimately score a perfect 10.00 for nongymnastic competitive behaviors?   It is the
opinion of the authors that the improvement of the human lot
could result if the incidence of certain behaviors changed from
what was observed in Montreal.

For instance, would it not be simple to obliterate the nearly
33% of performances that are not rewarded with positive feedback
by the simple nod, touch, or smile of the coach or a teammate?
Would not the artistic communication process be more complete
between the gymnast and the judge or the audience if, after a well-
performed routine, the gymnast shared his or her joy rather than
wearing the mask of indifference 60% of the time?   While recog-
nizing the demands required in the search for excellence, would
it not be possible to voluntarily increase the human contact beyond .5% with teammates who are sharing these same moments of
high excitement?   Surely the payoffs for such small, but significant
behaviors are worth the low risks of sacrificing some real or
imaginary performance edge.

Overall, there were some interesting phenomena observed that
certainly open the door for further investigation.   For example,
were the different profiles in all four phases of the behavioral observations for the men and the women the result of real sex differences, or were they due to the difference in ages?   What does the
variation in behavioral profiles within different performance
brackets indicate about being a "winner" or a "loser"?   They
surely do not act in the same manner in the highest and lowest
performance echelons.   And what is it about life in the Soviet
Union that makes their gymnasts' behavior patterns so different
even from countries having close political and geographical affini-
ty or from others that can match their gymnastic performances?

The answers to these questions cannot be resolved only by con-
tinuing the observational process of future competitions, although
this would be interesting in determining the stability of these
phenomena.   There have to be additional measures of an experimental nature added to this observation process.   One method
would be the addition of rewards or punishments that would be
contingent upon an increase in the occurrence of desirable behaviors, as occurs in applied behavior analysis research (Baer,

Wolf, & Risley, 1968). In China, for example, these reinforcements are social in nature, as the gymnasts attempt to live up to their sports slogan "friendship first, competition second" (Salmela, 1979c). Another method of complementing this information would be through interviewing the athletes and asking them how they perceived the records of their behaviors, either in terms of their intensity or direction.

The observation process of situations in everyday life is a potentially rewarding one, although the efforts expended (and they are substantial) cannot guarantee benefits of the same magnitude. Nevertheless, the potentiality seems enormous for controlled experimental investigation of other sport phenomena as a function of sex, task difficulty, performance levels, or culture of performer origin, using the existing rubrics of sport psychology. The epilogue most fitting to this portrait of descriptive sport ethology, so as not to discourage further related undertakings, comes from Baer, Wolf, & Risley (1968), in their statement justifying further use of applied behavior analysis: "Consequently, the rate of displaying experimental control required of behavioral applications has become correspondingly less than standards typical of laboratory research. This is . . . because society rarely will allow its important behaviors, in their correspondingly important settings, to be manipulated repeatedly for the merely logical comfort of a scientifically skeptical audience" (p. 92).

REFERENCES

Alderman, R.B. *Psychological behavior in sport.* Philadelphia: Lea & Febiger, 1974.

Arend, S., & Higgins, J.R. A strategy for the classification, subjective analysis and observation of human movement. *Journal of Human Movement Studies,* 1976, *2,* 36–52.

Baer, D.M., M.M., & Risley, T.R. Some current dimensions of applied behavior analysis. *Journal of Applied Behavior Analysis,* 1968, *1,* 91–97.

Ball, D. Structural correlates of Olympic success. *International Journal of Comparative Sociology,* 1972, *13,* 186–200.

Bardwick, J.M. *Psychology of women.* New York: Harper & Row, 1971.

Bilodeau, I.M. Information feedback. In E.A. Bilodeau (Ed.), *Acquisition of skill.* New York: Academic Press, 1966.

Bouchard, C., Brunelle, J., & Godbout, P. *La préparation d'un champion.* Québec: Pélican, 1975.

Bouchard, C. Les déterminants de la performance au hockey. *Mouvement— Spécial Hockey 2,* 1975, 15–22.

Brown, R. *Social psychology.* New York: Free Press, 1965.

Broyard, A. Gender advertisements. *International Herald Tribune.* April 28–29, 1979, p. 12.

Brunelle, J., Talbot, S., Tousignant, M., Hubert, M., & Ouellet, C. Inventaire du comportement pédagogique des instructeurs de hockey en situation d'enseignement dans une perspective de supervision. In F. Landry and W.A.R. Orban (Eds.), *Psychology of sport, motor learning and didactics of physical activity* (Vol. 7). Miami: Symposia Specialists, 1978.

Carron, A.V. Personality and athletics: A review. In B.S. Rushall (Ed.), *The status of psycho-motor learning and sport psychology research.* Halifax: Sport Science Associates, 1975.

Cooper, L. Athletics, activity and personality: A review of the literature. *Research Quarterly,* 1969, *40,* 17–22.

Corbin, C.B. Mental practice. In W.P. Morgan (Ed.), *Ergogenic aids and muscular performance.* New York: Academic Press, 1972.

Cumming, G.R. *Fitness investigations at Pan-Am games.* Unpublished report, 1967.

Deci, E.L. *Intrinsic motivation.* New York: Plenum Press, 1975.

De Garay, A.L., Levine, L., & Carter, J.G.L. *Genetic and anthropological*

143

studies of Olympic athletes. New York: Academic Press, 1974.

Desharnais, R. The psychological aspects of archery. *Canadian Archery Association Publication.* Ottawa: Canadian Archery Association, 1976.

Dickenson, J. *A behavioral analysis of sport.* London: Lepus, 1977.

Eysenck, H. J. *Uses and abuses of psychology.* Baltimore: Penguin, 1953.

Frederick, A.B., & Wilson, M.U. Web graphics and the qualitative analysis of movement. *Kinesiology III* (Washington, D.C.: AAHPER), 1973, 1–11.

Franks, B.D. Physical warm-up. In W.P.Morgan (Ed.), *Ergogenic aids and muscular performance.* New York: Academic Press, 1972.

Genov, F. The nature and the mobilization readiness of the sportsman and the influence of different factors upon its formation. In G.S. Kenyon (Ed.), *Contemporary psychology of sport.* Washington: Athletic Institute, 1970.

George, G.S. *The biomechanics of women's gymnastics.* Englewood Cliffs, N.J.: Prentice-Hall, 1980.

Goffman, E. *Gender advertisements.* Cambridge, Mass.: Harvard University Press, 1979.

Gregory, C.J., & Petrie, B.M. Superstition in sport. *Proceedings of fourth Canadian symposium in psycho-motor learning and sport psychology,* Ottawa, 1973.

Hall, R.V. *Managing behavior. I: The measurement of behavior.* Laurence Kansas: H & H Enterprises, 1974.

Hallé, M. *Evaluation des comportements observables des gymnastes olympiques quatre minutes avant leur performance.* Unpublished masters thesis, Laval University, 1978.

Hanin, Y. Personal communication, Prague, 1977.

Harris, D. *Women and sport.* University Park, Pa.: Pennsylvania State University Press, 1972.

Kane, J.E. Cognitive aspects of performance. *British Journal of Sports Medicine,* 1978, *4,* 201–207.

Kane, J.E. Psychological aspects of sports with special reference to the female. In D. Harris (Ed.), *Women and sport.* University Park, Pa.: Pennsylvania State University Press, 1972.

Kazdin, A.G. *Behavior modification in applied settings.* Homewood, Ill.: Dorsey, 1975.

Kennicke, L. Masks of identity. In D. Harris (Ed.), *Women and sport.* University Park, Pa.: Pennsylvania State University Press, 1972.

Klavora, P. Emotional arousal in athletics: New considerations. In C. Bard, M. Fleury, & J.H. Salmela (Eds.), *Proceedings of the Seventh Canadian Psycho-motor Learning and Sport Psychology Symposium—Mouvement,* Montreal: APAPQ, 1975.

Lascari, A. Aesthetics and mechanics in artistic gymnastics and sport. In J.H. Salmela (Ed.), *The advanced study of gymnastics.* Springfield: Thomas, 1976.

Leveau, B., Ward, T., & Nelson, R.C. Body dimensions of Japanese and American gymnasts. *Medicine and Science in Sports,* 1974, *6,* 146–150.

Loken, N.C., & Willoughby, R.J. *The complete book of gymnastics* (5th ed.). Englewood Cliffs, N.J.: Prentice-Hall, 1977.

Luschen, G. *The cross-cultural analysis of sport and games.* Champaign, Ill.: Stipes, 1970.

Maehr, M.L. Toward a framework for the cross-cultural study of achievement motivation: McClelland reconsidered and redirected. In M.G. Wade & R. Martens (Eds.). *Psychology of motor behavior and sport.* Urbana, Ill.: Human Kinetics, 1974.

Martens, R. *Sport competition anxiety test.* Champaign, Ill.: Human Kinetics, 1977.

Martens, R. Trait and state anxiety. In W.P. Morgan (Ed.), *Ergogenic aids and muscular performance.* New York: Academic Press, 1972.

Medved, R. Body, height and predisposition for certain sports. *Journal of Sports Medicine and Physical Fitness,* 1966, *6,* 95–105.

Metheney, E. *Connotations of movement in sport and dance.* Dubuque, Iowa: Wm. C. Brown, 1965.

Montpetit, R.R. The physiology of gymnastics. In J.H. Salmela (Ed.), *The advanced study of gymnastics.* Springfield: Thomas, 1976.

Morgan, W.P. *Ergogenic aids and muscular performance.* New York: Academic Press, 1972.

Morton, H.W. *Soviet sport.* New York: Collier, 1970.

Neal, P.E., & Tutko, T.A. *Coaching girls and women: psychological perspectives.* Boston: Allyn & Bacon, 1975.

Nelson, R.C. Comparison of body dimensions of Japanese, Hungarian and American gymnasts. *Gymnast,* 1974, *10,* 44–46.

Neuberger, T. What the Research Quarterly says about warm-up. *Journal of Health, Physical Education and Recreation,* 1969, *40,* 75–77.

Nideffer, R.M. *The inner athlete.* New York: Crowell, 1976.

Ogilvie, B.C. What is an athlete? *Journal of Health, Physical Education and Recreation,* 1967 (6), 48.

Orlick, T.D. Psychological circles in gymnastics. In J.H. Salmela (Ed.), *The advanced study of gymnastics.* Springfield: Thomas, 1976.

Orlick, T.D. *Winning through cooperation.* Washington: Hawkins, 1978.

Parizkova, J. La masse active, la graisse déposée et la constitution corporelle chez les sportifs de haut niveau. *Kinanthropologie,* 1972, *4,* 95–106.

Régnier, G., & Salmela, J.H. Perceptual determinants of gymnastic performance: Developmental considerations. In P. Klavora (Ed.), *Biomechanical and motor learning contributions to sport.* Toronto: University of Toronto 1980.

Restak, R.M. *The brain: The last frontier.* New York: Doubleday, 1979.

Roberts, G. C. Win-loss attributions of little league players. In C. Bard,

M. Fleury, & J.H. Salmela (Eds.), *Actes du septième symposium Canadien en apprentissage moteur et an psychologie du sport—Mouvement.* Montréal: APAPQ, 1975.

Roberts, J.M., & Sutton-Smith, B.   Cross-cultural correlates of games of chance. *Behavioral Science Notes,* 1966, *3,* 131–144.

Roethlisberger, F.A.   *Socialization of elite gymnasts.*   Unpublished masters thesis, University of Wisconsin, 1970.

Rushall, B.S.   The bases for advocating applied behavior analysis as a psychology for practitioners.   In D.M. Landers & R.W. Christina (Eds.), *Psychology of motor behavior and sport.*   Champaign, Ill.: Human Kinetics, 1978.

Rushall, B.S., & Siedentop, D.   *The development and control of behavior in sport.*   Philadelphia: Lea & Febiger, 1972.

Salmela, J.H.   Psycho-motor task demands of gymnastics.   In J.H. Salmela (Ed.), *The advanced study of gymnastics.*   Springfield: Thomas, 1976. (a)

Salmela, J.H.   *The advanced study of gymnastics.*   Springfield: Thomas, 1976. (b)

Salmela, J.H.   The psychology of competitive gymnastics: Psycho-motor learning and sport psychology considerations.   *CGF Coaching Certification Programme—level II.*   Otttawa: Canadian Gymnastics Federation, 1977.

Salmela, J.H.   A cross-cultural assessment of pre– and post-competitive behaviors of Olympic gymnasts.   In M. Vanek (Ed.), *IV Svetovy kongress ISSP,* Prague, 1979.

Salmela, J.H.   Down to the ground: Feedback for Olympic gymnasts upon dismounting. *Journal of Human Movement Studies,* 1979, (b) *5,* 77–89.

Salmela, J.H.   Gymnastic skill learning in China.   *Coaching Review,* 1979, *2,* 32–36. (c)

Salmela, J.H.   Growth patterns of elite French-Canadian gymnasts. *Canadian Journal of Applied Sport Sciences,* 1979, *3.* (d)

Salmela, J.H.   On falling off the pommel horse.   *International Gymnast,* 1979, *6,* 70–71. (e)

Salmela, J.H.   Training for competitive gymnastics.   In H. Straus (Ed), *Gymnastics Guide.*   Mountain View, Ca.: World Publications, 1979, 140–145. (f)

Salmela, J.H., Hallé, M., Petiot, B. & Samson, R.   Determinants of Olympic gymnastic performance.   In F. Landry and W.A.R. Orban (Eds.), *Psychology of sport, motor learning and didactics of physical activity* (Vol 7). Miami: Symposia Specialists, 1978.

Salmela, J.H., Janssen, L.P., Pilvein, M., & Dasalva, A. Psychological management of top athletes. *International Journal of Sport Psychology,* 1979, *10,* 156-163.

Salmela, J.H., & Lavoie, G.   Speed and accuracy characteristics of manual releases during gymnastic pommel horse performance.   In D.M. Landers

& R.W. Christina (Eds.), *Psychology of motor behavior and sport* (Vol. 1). Urbana, Ill.: Human Kinetics, 1977.

Salmela, J.H., Petiot, B., Hallé, M., Samson, R., & Biesterfeldt, J. Psychological compatibility: Gymnast and his event. In L. Sinclair (Ed.), *Everything that you wanted to know about gymnastics* . . . . Ottawa: Canadian Gymnastics Federation, 1980.

Salmela, J.H., Régnier, G. & Proteau, L. Predicteurs de le performance gymnique. *Premier colloque international sur la médicine de la gymnastique.* Paris: Economica, 1979.

Sandle, D. Aesthetics and the psychology of qualitative movement. In J.E. Kane (Ed.), *Psychological aspects of physical education and sport.* London: Routledge and Kegan Paul, 1172.

Sherif, C. Females in the competitive process. In D. Harris (Ed.), *Women and sport.* University Park, Pa.: Pennsylvania State University Press, 1972.

Sidman, M. *Tactics of scientific research.* New York: Basic Books, 1960.

Smith, R.F., Smoll, F.L., & Hunt, E. A system for the behavioral assessment of athletic coaches. *Research Quarterly,* 1977, *48,* 401–407.

Smoll, F., Smith, R., & Hunt, E. *Behavioral assessment in little league baseball.* Paper presented at the Symposium on Contemporary Research in Youth Sports, Seattle, March 1977.

Spielberger, C. D. Theory and research on anxiety. In C.D. Spielberger (Ed.), *Anxiety and behavior.* New York: Academic Press, 1966.

Stuart, N. *Competitive gymnastics.* London: Stanley Paul, 1964.

Taylor, A.W. *The scientific aspects of sports training.* Springfield: Thomas, 1975.

Tharp, R.G., & Gallimore, R. What a coach can teach a teacher. *Psychology Today,* 1976, *1,* 75–78.

Vanek, M., & Cratty, B.J. *Psychology and the superior athlete.* London: Macmillan, 1970.

Vanek, M., Hosek, V., & Svoboda, B. *Studie osobnosti ve sportu.* Prague: Universita Karlova, 1974.

Weiner, B. *Achievement motivation and attribution theory.* Morristown, N.J.: General Learning Press, 1974.

Wolcott, H. Criteria for an ethnographic approach to research in schools. *Human Organization,* 1975, *34,* 111–127.

Zoble, J., Femininity and achievement in sports. In D. Harris (Ed.), *Women and sport.* University Park, Pa.: Pennsylania State University Press, 1972.

AUTHOR INDEX

SUBJECT INDEX